Cycle
Tours

Hampshire & the Isle of Wight

Nick Cotton

Publisher: Cycle Tours is a joint venture between
CycleCity Guides and Cordee

CycleCity Guides
The Welsh Mill
Parkhill Drive
Frome
BA11 2LE
T: +44 (0)1373 453533

info@cyclecityguides.co.uk
www.cyclecityguides.co.uk

Cordee
11 Jacknell Road
Dodwells Bridge Industrial Estate
Hinckley
LE10 3BS
T: +44 (0)1455 611 185

charlie@cordee.co.uk
www.cordee.co.uk

ISBN: 978 1 904207 52 8

Printed by: Kingsdown
Picture credits: Nick Cotton

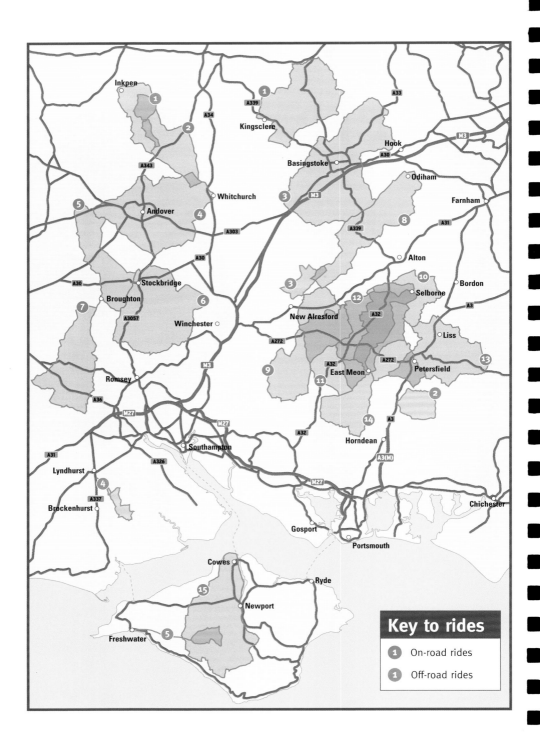

Key to rides

1 On-road rides

1 Off-road rides

Quick reference chart

On-road rides

Ride number & title	Page	Distance	Grade
1 Kingsclere to the old Roman walls of Silchester	8	30m (48km)	▲▲
2 Whitchurch & the North Hampshire Downs	14	33m (53km)	▲▲▲▲
3 A ring around Basingstoke from Old Basing	20	40m (64km)	▲▲
4 A ring around Andover from Whitchurch	26	32m (52km)	▲
5 Stockbridge, Thruxton & the Wallops	32	28m (45km)	▲
6 Stockbridge & the Test Valley	38	30m (48km)	▲▲
7 From Broughton to the edge of the New Forest	44	32m (52km)	▲▲
8 New Alresford to Odiham	50	38m (61km)	▲▲▲
9 Above the Meon Valley south of New Alresford	56	30m (48km)	▲▲▲
10 East Meon north to Farringdon	62	33m (53km)	▲▲▲▲
11 From Selborne to the Meon Valley & Cheriton	68	37m (60km)	▲▲▲▲
12 Petersfield & the Meon Valley	74	35m (56km)	▲▲▲▲
13 Wooded lanes through the Rother Valley from Buriton	80	28m (45km)	▲▲
14 East Meon south to Hambledon	86	23m (37km)	▲▲▲
15 Around the Isle of Wight on railway paths & quiet roads	92	34m (55km)	▲▲▲

Off-road rides

Ride number & title	Page	Distance	Grade
1 Hurstbourne Tarrant & Inkpen Hill	98	17m (27km)	▲▲▲▲
2 Queen Elizabeth Country Park & the South Downs Way	102	10m (16km)	▲▲▲
3 Rolling Hampshire downland from New Alresford	106	12m (19km)	▲▲
4 New Forest tracks from Lyndhurst	110	13m (21km)	▲
5 The Tennyson Trail on the Isle of Wight	114	20m (32km)	▲▲▲▲▲

Grades

▲	Easy
▲▲	Easy / Moderate
▲▲▲	Moderate
▲▲▲▲	Moderate / Strenuous
▲▲▲▲▲	Strenuous

The grade is based on the amount of climbing involved and, for off-road routes, the roughness of the surface rather than the distance covered.

1

Hampshire & Isle of Wight

The rolling chalk downland of Hampshire and the Isle of Wight offer some splendid cycling both on the network of quiet lanes linking attractive villages, and also on the broad chalk and flint byways and bridleways that criss-cross the area.

In the north of Hampshire the land rises to 975ft (297m) on Walbury Hill, the highest chalk downland in the country. One of the two rides from Whitchurch explores this area with its fine views over the Kennet Valley. The other describes a circuit around Andover passing through myriad pretty villages full of thatched houses. Three road rides are based in or near Stockbridge on the River Test,

the famous fishing river. One heads southwest to the edge of the New Forest, an area best explored on its off-road tracks.

Two rides start from New Alresford, one of the most handsome towns in Hampshire with its wide streets and many Georgian buildings. The ride that heads south from here overlaps with several others that explore one of the most wonderful areas in the county for lane cycling – the area lying in a 10-mile radius around the pretty village of East Meon. Almost every lane is a delight at any time of the year.

Finally, for the road rides, the Isle of Wight is explored to the southwest of Cowes, using

two of the island's top-quality railway paths.

The off-road rides are widely spread: the easiest one uses easy gravel tracks through the New Forest to the southeast of Lyndhurst; the toughest is a magnificent chalk ridge ride along the Tennyson Trail on the Isle of Wight with fine views over the Solent and out into the English Channel. A third starts from Queen Elizabeth Country Park near Petersfield, a real mecca for mountain bikers. To the north of New Alresford there is a network of broad, easy chalk tracks best explored after a dry spell in summer; the final ride climbs up onto Inkpen Hill and uses tough woodland singletrack with some swooping descents.

Other useful information

Easy, traffic-free cycling for families and novices

If you want a ride that is also suitable for children or 'novice' cyclists try some of these easier traffic-free routes on dismantled railways, canal towpaths or in Forestry Commission holdings. Hampshire County Council's general cycling website is **www.hants.gov.uk/cycling**

1. The Test Way (5 miles)
Starting near the roundabout at the east end of Stockbridge High Street, this railway path runs south to Mottisfont. Go to **www.hants.gov.uk/cycling**, click on **'Find routes to ride my bike'** then click on **'Test Way'**.

2. New Forest (many routes)
The New Forest is criss-crossed by tracks. Go to **www.hants.gov.uk/cycling** and click on **'New Forest'**. Alternatively, try the other New Forest websites listed under Off-road Route 4 (page 110).

3. Meon Valley Trail (10 miles)
Running from West Meon south to Wickham, near Fareham, this railway path is now only suitable for mountain bikes as it gets very muddy. Best in summer after a long dry spell:
http://homepage.ntlworld.com/ron.strutt/rrcor3.html

4. Basingstoke Canal (15 miles)
The Hampshire section of this lovely canal towpath runs from Ash / Aldershot west through Fleet to North Warnborough: **www.basingstoke-canal.org.uk**

5. Alice Holt Forest, southwest of Farnham (4 miles)
An easy waymarked route on broad forest tracks:
www.forestry.gov.uk/england-cycling and click on **'Alice Holt'**.

6. Queen Elizabeth Country Park, southwest of Petersfield (4 miles)
Forestry Commission holding with waymarked routes, although the terrain is fairly hilly:
www3.hants.gov.uk/qecp click on **'Park activities'** then **'Cycling'**.

Isle of Wight

There are four railway paths on the Isle of Wight:
1. Yarmouth to Freshwater (3 miles)

2. Cowes to Newport (3 miles)

3. Newport to Sandown (7 miles)

4. Shanklin to Wroxall (2 miles)

www.cyclewight.org.uk

Sustrans and the National Cycle Network

Go to **www.sustrans.org.uk**, click on **'Sustrans near you'** then **'South East'** then **'Hampshire and the Isle of Wight'**. There are downloads, details of free leaflets and details of NCN routes in the region.

Cycle shops in the area
www.ihampshire.co.uk/local/cycle-shops/
www.thecyclepeople.com

Legend to 1:50,000 maps

Roads & paths

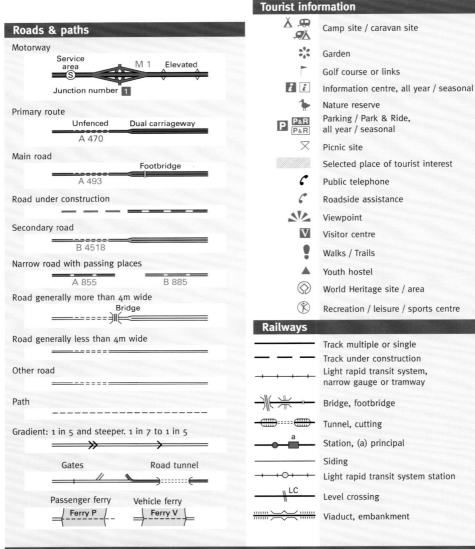

Motorway

Service area (S) M 1 Elevated

Junction number [1]

Primary route

Unfenced   Dual carriageway
A 470

Main road

Footbridge
A 493

Road under construction

Secondary road
B 4518

Narrow road with passing places
A 855   B 885

Road generally more than 4m wide
Bridge

Road generally less than 4m wide

Other road

Path

Gradient: 1 in 5 and steeper. 1 in 7 to 1 in 5

Gates   Road tunnel

Passenger ferry   Vehicle ferry
Ferry P   Ferry V

Tourist information

Ⓧ ⚏ ⚐   Camp site / caravan site

✻   Garden

⚑   Golf course or links

i [i]   Information centre, all year / seasonal

🦆   Nature reserve

P P&R P&R   Parking / Park & Ride, all year / seasonal

✕   Picnic site

▨▨▨   Selected place of tourist interest

✆   Public telephone

✆   Roadside assistance

☀   Viewpoint

V   Visitor centre

❗   Walks / Trails

▲   Youth hostel

⊛   World Heritage site / area

⊗   Recreation / leisure / sports centre

Railways

—————   Track multiple or single

— — —   Track under construction

┼┼┼┼   Light rapid transit system, narrow gauge or tramway

Bridge, footbridge

Tunnel, cutting

Station, (a) principal

Siding

Light rapid transit system station

LC   Level crossing

Viaduct, embankment

Water features

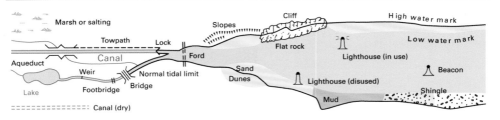

Marsh or salting

Towpath   Lock

Canal

Aqueduct

Weir   Normal tidal limit

Lake   Footbridge   Bridge

Ford

Slopes   Cliff   High water mark

Flat rock   Low water mark

Sand   Dunes   Lighthouse (in use)

Mud   Lighthouse (disused)   Beacon

Shingle

Canal (dry)

4

General features

¦¦¦¦¦ ¦¦¦¦¦	Cutting, embankment
	Landfill site
	Coniferous wood
	Non-coniferous wood
	Mixed wood
	Orchard
	Park or ornamental ground
	Forestry Commission land
	National Trust - always open
	National Trust - limited access, observe local signs
	National Trust for Scotland - always open
	National Trust for Scotland - limited access, observe local signs
∧ ∧ ∧	Electricity transmission line (pylons shown at standard spacing)
> - -> - ->	Pipe line (arrow indicates direction of flow)
ruin	Building
	Important building (selected)
	Bus or coach station
	Glass structure
Ⓗ	Hospital
	Place of worship with tower
	Place of worship with spire, dome or minaret
+	Place of worship
	Mast
	Wind pump / wind turbine
	Windmill with or without sails
+	Graticule intersection at 5' intervals

Rock features

Outcrop Cliff Scree

Public rights of way
(not applicable in Scotland)

----------------	Footpath
-·-·-·-·-·-	Restricted byway
--------	Bridleway
-+-+-+-+-+-	Byway open to all traffic

Public rights of way shown have been taken from local authority definitive maps and later amendments. The symbols show the defined route so far as the scale of mapping will allow.

The representation on this map of any other road, track or path is no evidence of the existence of a right of way.

Other public access

· · · ·	Other route with public access
◆ ◆ ◆	National Trail, European Long Distance Path, Long Distance Route, selected Recreational Routes
● ● ●	On-road cycle route
○ ○ ○	Off-road cycle route
4	National Cycle Network Number
8	Regional Cycle Network Number
Danger Area	Firing and test ranges in the area Danger! Observe warning notices

Boundaries

+ — + — +	National
-+-·-+-·-+-	District
—·—··—··—	County, region or island area
	National Park

Abbreviations

CH	Clubhouse
PH	Public house
PC	Public convenience (in rural area)
TH	Town Hall, Guildhall or equivalent
CG	Cattle grid
P	Post office
MP	Milepost
MS	Mile stone

Antiquities

+	Position of antiquity that cannot be drawn to scale
☆ ····	Visible earthwork
VILLA	Roman
Castle	Non-Roman
✕	Battlefield (with date)

Heights

═══50═══	Contours are at 10 metre vertical intervals
·144	Heights are to the nearest metre above mean sea level
	Heights shown close to a triangulation pillar refer to the station height at ground level and not necessarily to the summit

Abbreviations and instructions

Instructions are given concisely to make them easy to follow while out riding. Remember to read one or two instructions ahead so that you do not miss a turning. This is most likely when you have to turn off a road / track you have been following for a while and are marked **Easy to miss** to warn you.

If there appears to be a contradiction between the instructions and what you actually see, always refer to the map. There are many reasons why, over the course of time, instructions may be subject to change with new roads, new junctions and new signposts.

Directions (all directions are given in bold)

L	left
R	right
SA	straight ahead
bear **L** or **R**	a turn which is less than 90 degrees (right-angle) at a fork in the road or on a sharp bend so that your course appears to be straight ahead; this is often written as 'in effect **SA**'
sharp **L** or **R**	a turn more acute than a right-angle
L or **R** sharply back on yourself	almost a U-turn
R then **L**	normally a T-junction where the next turn is visible from the first
R then first **L**	the second turning may be some distance from the first, ie '**R** then after $1/2$ mile first **L**'

Junctions

T-j	T-junction, a junction where you have to give way
X-roads	crossroads, a junction where you may or may not have to give way
offset X-roads	the four roads are not in the form of a perfect cross and you will have to turn left then right, or vice versa, to continue the route

Signs

'Placename 2'	the words in quotation marks are those that appear on the signs, the numbers indicate the distance in miles unless stated otherwise
(NS)	not signposted

Instructions

An example of an easy instruction is:

4 At T-j at end of Smith Road by the White Swan Inn turn **R** on Brown Street 'Greentown 2, Redville 3'

There is more information in this instruction than you would normally need but things do change: pubs may close down and signs may be replaced, removed or vandalised.

An example of a difficult instruction is:

8 **Easy to miss:** shortly after the brow of the hill, on fast descent, first **R** (NS)

As you can see, there is no T-junction or 'Give Way' sign to halt you in your tracks, no signpost indicating where the right turn will take you and in addition you are picking up speed on a downhill, so you need to have your wits about you not to miss the turning.

Overview pages

Start
This is the suggested start point, coinciding with Instruction 1 on the map. There is no reason why you should not start at another point if it is more convenient.

Busy roads
These rides aim to keep to an absolute minimum time spent on busy roads but there are sometimes unavoidable sections where lane networks do not neatly link together. These busy roads are mentioned so that you are mentally prepared to deal with traffic, especially if there are children or less experienced cyclists in the group.

Off-road sections (on-road rides)
Occasionally a short distance on a traffic-free cyclepath, bridleway, byway or unclassified road can offer an alternative to a busy road. As the surfaces are not sealed you may encounter puddles or muddy water, especially in winter or after prolonged rain.

Terrain
This brief description of the terrain covered by the route should be read in conjunction with the cross-profile diagram at the foot of the page to help you plan your journey.

Distance
The distance (shown in miles and kilometres) is, of course, that from the beginning to the end of the ride. However, if you wish to shorten the ride because of tiredness, mechanical problems, a change in the weather or simply lack of time then the maps enable you to do so.

Grade
There are five grades of difficulty:
Easy
Easy / Moderate
Moderate
Moderate / Strenuous
Strenuous
The grade is based on the amount of climbing involved and, for off-road routes, the roughness of the surface rather than the distance covered.

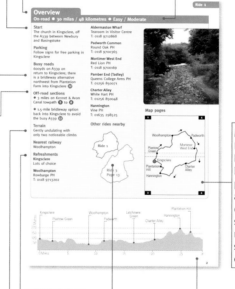

Map pages
Route overviews show how the maps have been laid out on the pages. Page numbers are shown in the corners. The diagrams show start points, route direction and some of the villages on or near the route.

Other rides nearby
Schematic map showing where nearby rides overlap. Shorter or longer rides can be created by mixing and matching rides.

Cross-profile
Shows heights in metres and distance travelled. Places along the route are shown.

Refreshments
More than three pubs or a mixture of pubs, cafés and tearooms in any one place is indicated by 'Lots of choice'. Otherwise, names of pubs, cafés and tearooms are listed, where possible with telephone numbers so that you can call ahead to check on opening times and when food is served.

Kingsclere to the old Roman walls of Silchester

The ride starts from the pretty town of Kingsclere and heads north, dropping down from Brimpton Common into the valley formed by the River Kennet, joining the towpath of the Kennet & Avon Canal for almost three miles between Woolhampton and Aldermaston Wharf. The Kennet & Avon Canal, linking Bristol and Reading, was built in three sections. The stretch from Reading to Newbury was the earliest of the three (1718-23) and involved the building of 18 locks in as many miles to raise the canal 138ft. The section from Newbury west to Bath was not opened until 1810, almost 90 years later. Leave the canal and climb south through Padworth and Mortimer West End to the old Roman settlement of Silchester. Lying at a junction of five Roman roads, Calleva Atrebatum was a rich wool-trading town and a provincial administrative centre with a population of 4,000 in the Roman era. A 2-mile section of wall still remains, well worth closer inspection. Imagine leaving Italy, marching a couple of thousand miles north to England and being told to build a massive town wall near Basingstoke. Skirting around Tadley, the ride climbs up onto the North Hampshire Downs to a highpoint of 660ft (201m) in Hannington.

Warning: If you stay on-road you will have to cope with an unpleasant 600yds on the busy A339 close to the end of the ride. There is a stone-based bridleway as an alternative back into Kingsclere.

Overview

On-road ● 30 miles / 48 kilometres ● Easy / Moderate

Start
The church in Kingsclere, off the A339 between Newbury and Basingstoke

Parking
Follow signs for free parking in Kingsclere

Busy roads
600yds on A339 on return to Kingsclere; there is a bridleway alternative northwest from Plantation Farm into Kingsclere **22**

Off-road sections
● 3 miles on Kennet & Avon Canal towpath **5** to **8**

● 1.5-mile bridleway option back into Kingsclere to avoid the busy A339 **22**

Terrain
Gently undulating with only two noticeable climbs

Nearest railway
Woolhampton

Refreshments
Kingsclere
Lots of choice

Woolhampton
Rowbarge PH
T: 0118 9713202

Aldermaston Wharf
Tearoom in Visitor Centre
T: 0118 9712868

Padworth Common
Round Oak PH
T: 0118 9700365

Mortimer West End
Red Lion PH
T: 0118 9700169

Pamber End (Tadley)
Queens College Arms PH
T: 01256 850071

Charter Alley
White Hart PH
T: 01256 850048

Hannington
Vine PH
T: 01635 298525

Other rides nearby

Map pages

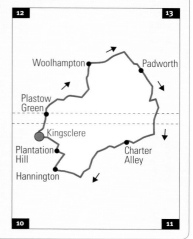

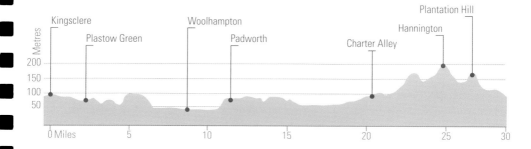

9

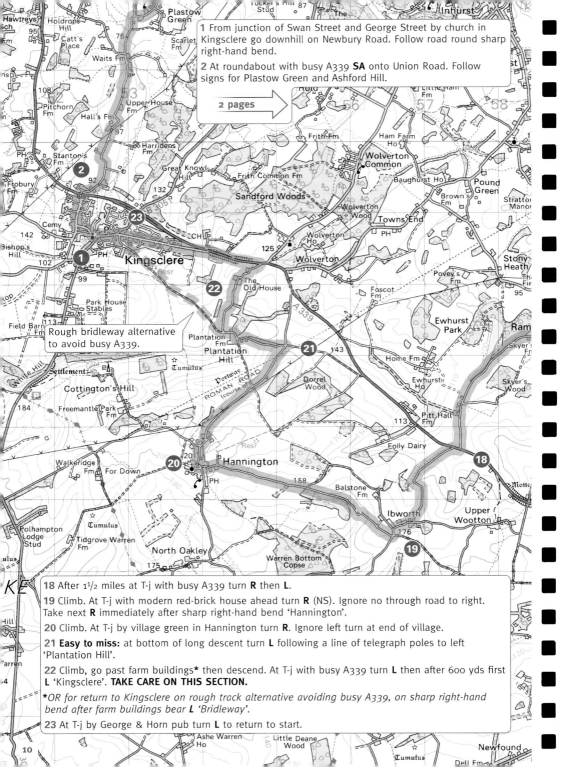

1 From junction of Swan Street and George Street by church in Kingsclere go downhill on Newbury Road. Follow road round sharp right-hand bend.

2 At roundabout with busy A339 **SA** onto Union Road. Follow signs for Plastow Green and Ashford Hill.

2 pages →

Rough bridleway alternative to avoid busy A339.

18 After 1½ miles at T-j with busy A339 turn **R** then **L**.

19 Climb. At T-j with modern red-brick house ahead turn **R** (NS). Ignore no through road to right. Take next **R** immediately after sharp right-hand bend 'Hannington'.

20 Climb. At T-j by village green in Hannington turn **R**. Ignore left turn at end of village.

21 **Easy to miss:** at bottom of long descent turn **L** following a line of telegraph poles to left 'Plantation Hill'.

22 Climb, go past farm buildings* then descend. At T-j with busy A339 turn **L** then after 600 yds first **L** 'Kingsclere'. **TAKE CARE ON THIS SECTION.**

*OR for return to Kingsclere on rough track alternative avoiding busy A339, on sharp right-hand bend after farm buildings bear **L** 'Bridleway'.

23 At T-j by George & Horn pub turn **L** to return to start.

10

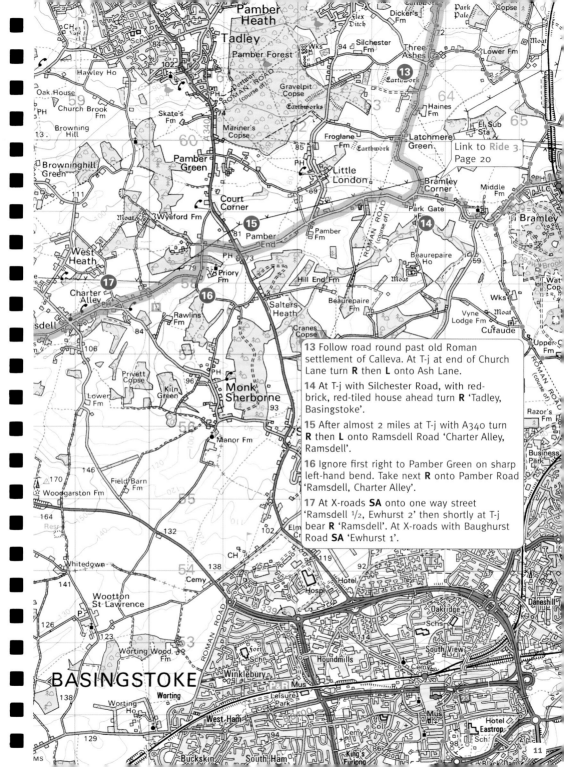

13 Follow road round past old Roman settlement of Calleva. At T-j at end of Church Lane turn **R** then **L** onto Ash Lane.

14 At T-j with Silchester Road, with red-brick, red-tiled house ahead turn **R** 'Tadley, Basingstoke'.

15 After almost 2 miles at T-j with A340 turn **R** then **L** onto Ramsdell Road 'Charter Alley, Ramsdell'.

16 Ignore first right to Pamber Green on sharp left-hand bend. Take next **R** onto Pamber Road 'Ramsdell, Charter Alley'.

17 At X-roads **SA** onto one way street 'Ramsdell ½, Ewhurst 2' then shortly at T-j bear **R** 'Ramsdell'. At X-roads with Baughurst Road **SA** 'Ewhurst 1'.

Link to **Ride 3**. Page 20

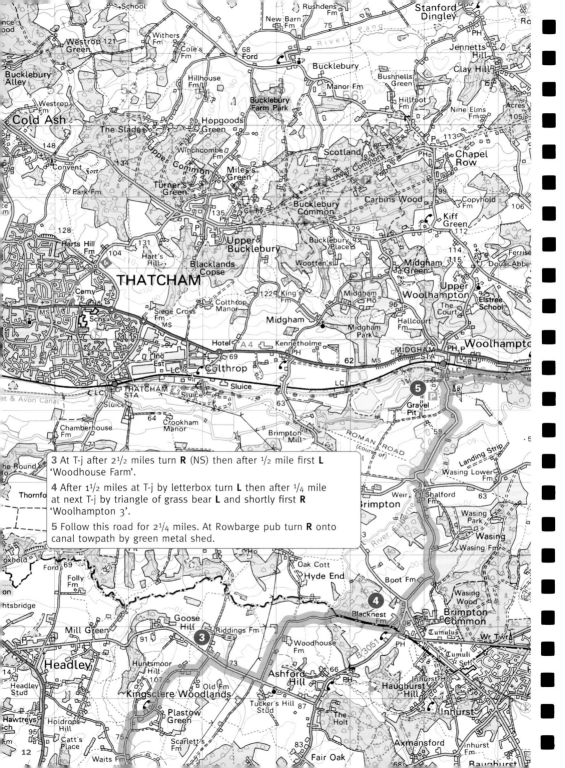

3 At T-j after 2¹/₂ miles turn **R** (NS) then after ¹/₂ mile first **L** 'Woodhouse Farm'.

4 After 1¹/₂ miles at T-j by letterbox turn **L** then after ¹/₄ mile at next T-j by triangle of grass bear **L** and shortly first **R** 'Woolhampton 3'.

5 Follow this road for 2¹/₄ miles. At Rowbarge pub turn **R** onto canal towpath by green metal shed.

6 At next road, after 1¼ miles, turn **R** then **L** to continue on towpath.

7 At T-j with road by red and white barriers and sign for Butt Inn turn **L** then **R**. Go past Visitor Centre and tearoom.

8 At low grey and white metal bridge after ½ mile turn **R** and leave towpath.

9 Climb gently for 1 mile then take first **L** at X-roads onto School Road 'The Ark School, Single Track Road'.

10 After 1¼ miles at X-roads **SA** 'Mortimer West End 1, Silchester 2½' (Round Oak pub is 100 yds to right).

11 Busier road. At T-j at end of Ramptons Lane turn **L** 'Silchester' then after 250 yds **R** onto Church Road 'Silchester'.

12 After 1 mile, on right-hand bend turn **L** onto Wall Lane '12th century church, Stratfield Saye'.

13 Follow road round past old Roman settlement of Calleva. At T-j at end of Church Lane turn **R** then **L** onto Ash Lane.

2 pages

Whitchurch & the North Hampshire Downs

The North Hampshire Downs are the highest chalk hills in Southern England, rising to a mighty 975ft (297m) on Walbury Hill, to the south of Hungerford. As might be expected, the views north from here on a fine, clear day are truly stunning, looking across the valley of the River Kennet towards the Lambourn Downs away to the north. The views are not unlike those from the South Downs ridge looking north into the Sussex Weald. The first half of the ride offers quite a contrast to this as you follow the valley of the River Bourne (or 'Bourne Rivulet' as it is shown on the map), through a series of picturesque, thatched villages and past watercress beds, which thrive in the clear-flowing chalk streams. The gradient steepens soon after passing through Upton, climbing to the first highpoint of the ride on the escarpment above Ham. After dropping down off the top there are opportunities for refreshments in Ham and Lower Green before the toughest climb of the day up to the masts on Combe Hill, with one very steep section near the top of the escarpment. If you need an excuse, stop and look behind you – the views are huge. After an unavoidable 400yds spell on the busy A343 beyond Ashmansworth, you are rewarded with a long and wonderful gentle descent of almost 5 miles on a lovely quiet lane almost right back to Whitchurch, where you may wish to visit its famous Silk Mill.

Overview

On-road ● 33 miles / 53 kilometres ● Moderate / Strenuous

Start
Roundabout in the centre of
Whitchurch, off the A34 south of
Newbury

Parking
Follow signs for free car park in
centre of Whitchurch

Busy roads
400yds (uphill) on the A343
near Ashmansworth with a
tricky right turn **15**

Off-road sections
None

Terrain
Hilly for Hampshire!

Nearest railway
Whitchurch

Refreshments
Whitchurch
Lots of choice

St Mary Bourne
George Inn
T: 01264 738340
Bourne Valley Inn
T: 01264 738361
Coronation Arms PH
T: 01264 738432

Hurstbourne Tarrant
George & Dragon PH
T: 01264 736277

Upton
Crown Inn
T: 01264 736265

Ham
Crown & Anchor PH
T: 01488 668242

Lower Green (Inkpen)
Swan Inn
T: 01488 668326

Faccombe
Jack Russell PH
T: 01264 737315

Ashmansworth
Plough PH
T: 01635 253047

Other rides nearby

Ride 2

Ride 4
Page 26

Map pages

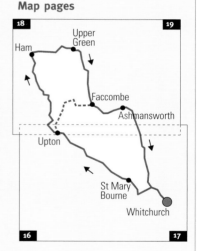

18 | 19
Ham
Upper Green
Faccombe
Ashmansworth
Upton
St Mary Bourne
Whitchurch
16 | 17

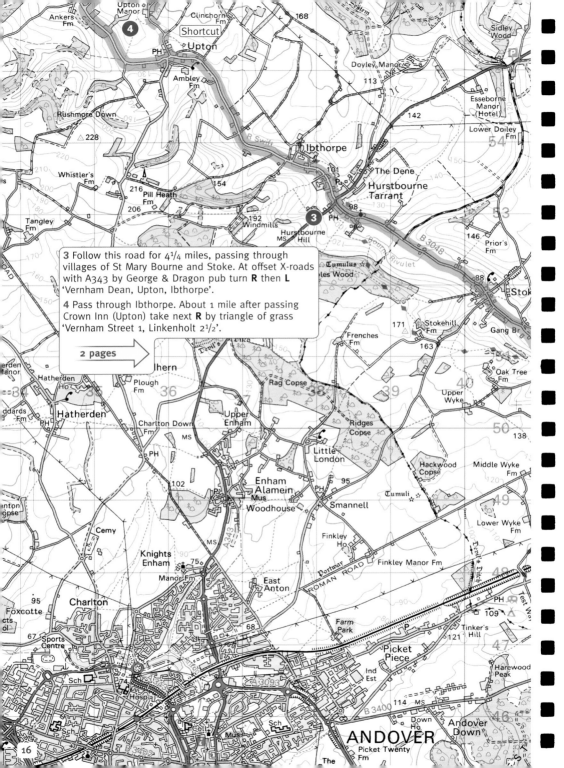

3 Follow this road for 4¼ miles, passing through villages of St Mary Bourne and Stoke. At offset X-roads with A343 by George & Dragon pub turn **R** then **L** 'Vernham Dean, Upton, Ibthorpe'.

4 Pass through Ibthorpe. About 1 mile after passing Crown Inn (Upton) take next **R** by triangle of grass 'Vernham Street 1, Linkenholt 2½'.

2 pages →

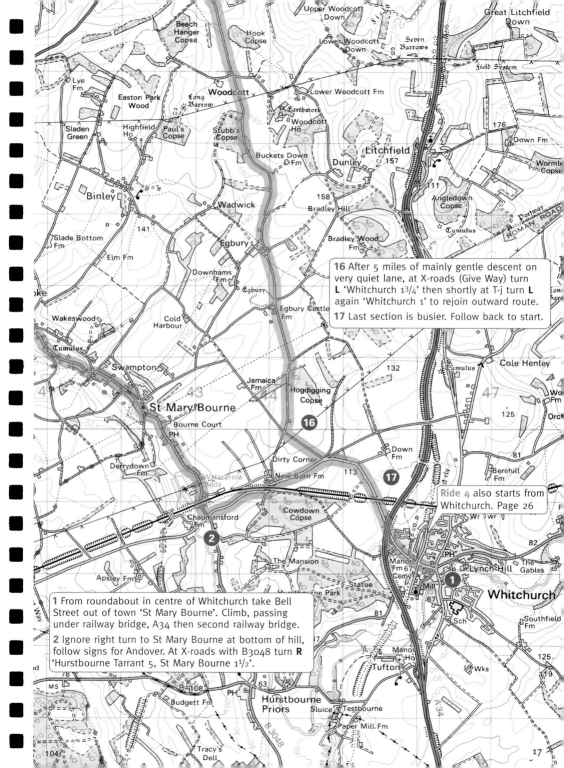

16 After 5 miles of mainly gentle descent on very quiet lane, at X-roads (Give Way) turn **L** 'Whitchurch 1¾' then shortly at T-j turn **L** again 'Whitchurch 1' to rejoin outward route.

17 Last section is busier. Follow back to start.

Ride 4 also starts from Whitchurch. Page 26

1 From roundabout in centre of Whitchurch take Bell Street out of town 'St Mary Bourne'. Climb, passing under railway bridge, A34 then second railway bridge.

2 Ignore right turn to St Mary Bourne at bottom of hill, follow signs for Andover. At X-roads with B3048 turn **R** 'Hurstbourne Tarrant 5, St Mary Bourne 1½'.

17

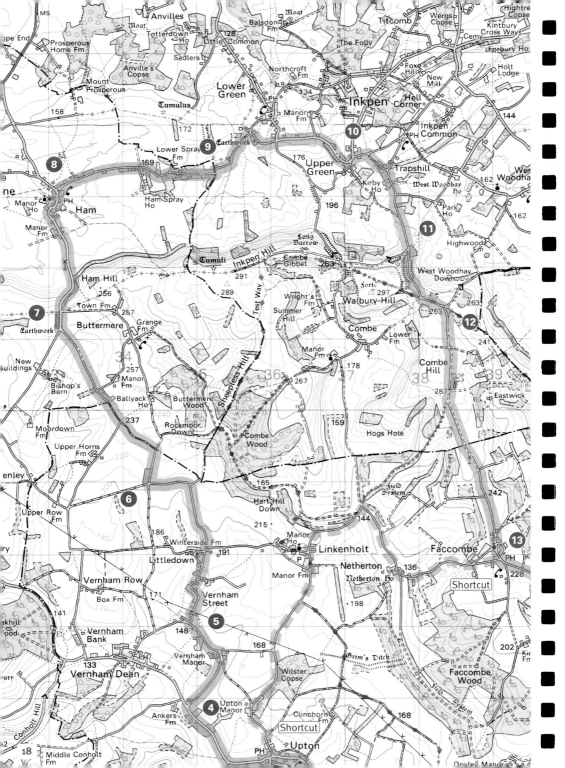

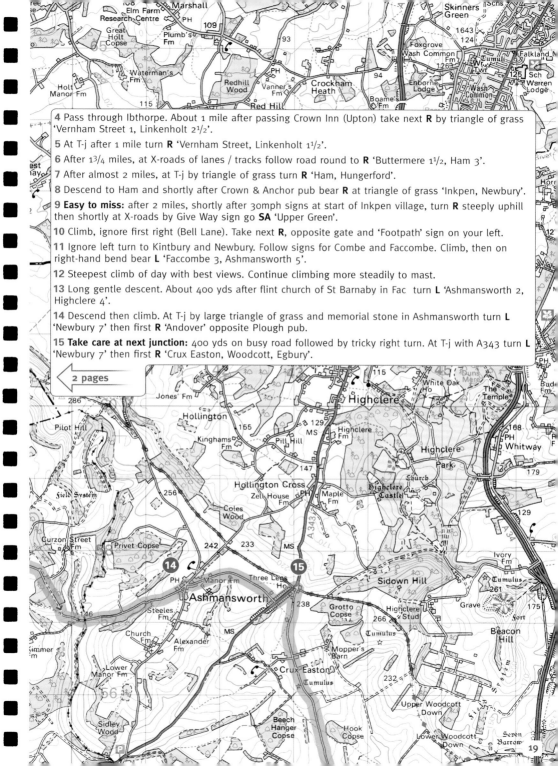

4 Pass through Ibthorpe. About 1 mile after passing Crown Inn (Upton) take next **R** by triangle of grass 'Vernham Street 1, Linkenholt 2½'.

5 At T-j after 1 mile turn **R** 'Vernham Street, Linkenholt 1½'.

6 After 1¾ miles, at X-roads of lanes / tracks follow road round to **R** 'Buttermere 1½, Ham 3'.

7 After almost 2 miles, at T-j by triangle of grass turn **R** 'Ham, Hungerford'.

8 Descend to Ham and shortly after Crown & Anchor pub bear **R** at triangle of grass 'Inkpen, Newbury'.

9 Easy to miss: after 2 miles, shortly after 30mph signs at start of Inkpen village, turn **R** steeply uphill then shortly at X-roads by Give Way sign go **SA** 'Upper Green'.

10 Climb, ignore first right (Bell Lane). Take next **R**, opposite gate and 'Footpath' sign on your left.

11 Ignore left turn to Kintbury and Newbury. Follow signs for Combe and Faccombe. Climb, then on right-hand bend bear **L** 'Faccombe 3, Ashmansworth 5'.

12 Steepest climb of day with best views. Continue climbing more steadily to mast.

13 Long gentle descent. About 400 yds after flint church of St Barnaby in Fac turn **L** 'Ashmansworth 2, Highclere 4'.

14 Descend then climb. At T-j by large triangle of grass and memorial stone in Ashmansworth turn **L** 'Newbury 7' then first **R** 'Andover' opposite Plough pub.

15 Take care at next junction: 400 yds on busy road followed by tricky right turn. At T-j with A343 turn **L** 'Newbury 7' then first **R** 'Crux Easton, Woodcott, Egbury'.

2 pages

A ring around Basingstoke from Old Basing

This is prosperous agricultural country with rolling fields of arable farmland forming the backdrop to much of the ride. Small areas of woodland with broadleaf deciduous trees give an indication of the chalk and clay geology and soil. Not unlike the next ride in the book, the circuit of Andover from Whitchurch, this ride crosses each of the roads radiating from the heart of Basingstoke like spokes from the hub of a wheel so that no time is spent on busy roads:

almost all the traffic is flowing in and out of the town on the arterial roads, leaving the parallel lanes relatively free of vehicles. It also means that anyone living in Basingstoke has the option of joining the circuit at the point closest to them, minimising time on urban roads. Although the longest ride in the book, it is far from the hardest as the land is gently rolling with no long or steep climbs. If you need a dose of culture, the ride goes right past the National Trust property of The

Vyne (between Bramley and Sherborne St John). Its three wings form an E-shaped red-brick Tudor mansion, set by a lake next to the River Loddon. There is superb Flemish stained glass and Italian glazed floor tiles in the Tudor chapel and fine oak panelling in the long gallery. The 16th century house is set in a large country park with gardens, lake, meadows, woods and wetlands.

Overview

On-road ● 40 miles / 64 kilometres ● Easy / Moderate

Start
The church in Old Basing, just to the east of Basingstoke

Parking
No specific car park. Some spaces near church. Alternatively park in the car park for Basing House, which lies less than 1/2 mile to the south (follow signs)

Busy roads
1/2 mile on the B3400 east of Oakley

Off-road sections
None

Terrain
Gently undulating with many short climbs of 100-200ft (30-60m) but no major hills

Nearest railway
Bramley

Refreshments
Old Basing
Lots of choice

Newnham
Old House at Home PH
T: 01256 762222

Lyde Green
Fox PH
T: 01256 882279

Stratfield Turgis
Wellington Arms Hotel
T: 01256 882214

Stratfield Saye
New Inn
T: 0118 9332255

Sherborne St John
Swan PH
T: 01256 850165

North Waltham (A30)
Wheatsheaf PH
T: 01256 398282

Axford
Crown PH
T: 01256 389492

Other rides nearby

Ride 1
Page 8

Ride 3

Ride 8
Page 50

Map pages

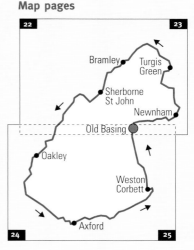

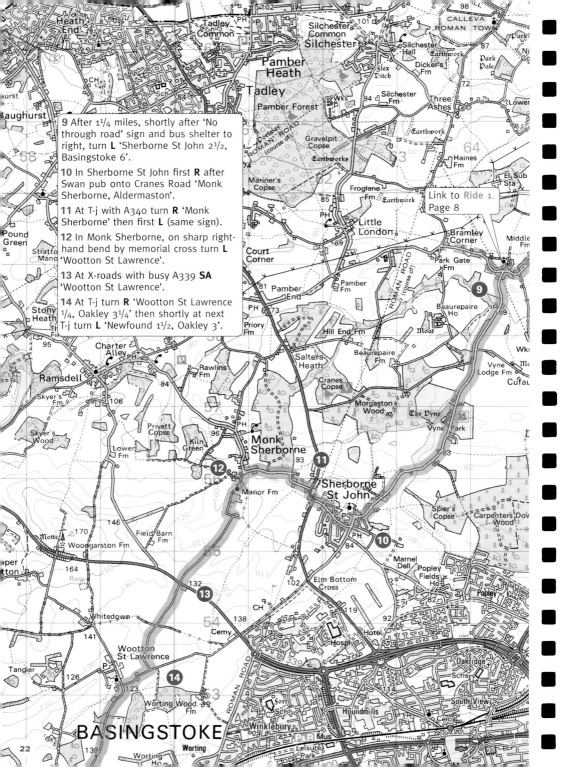

9 After 1¼ miles, shortly after 'No through road' sign and bus shelter to right, turn **L** 'Sherborne St John 2½, Basingstoke 6'.

10 In Sherborne St John first **R** after Swan pub onto Cranes Road 'Monk Sherborne, Aldermaston'.

11 At T-j with A340 turn **R** 'Monk Sherborne' then first **L** (same sign).

12 In Monk Sherborne, on sharp right-hand bend by memorial cross turn **L** 'Wootton St Lawrence'.

13 At X-roads with busy A339 **SA** 'Wootton St Lawrence'.

14 At T-j turn **R** 'Wootton St Lawrence ¼, Oakley 3¼' then shortly at next T-j turn **L** 'Newfound 1½, Oakley 3'.

Link to **Ride 1**. Page 8

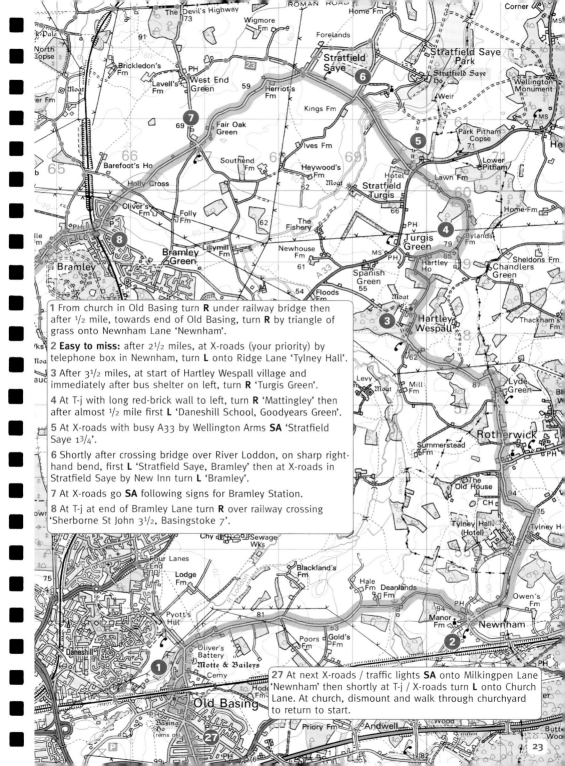

1 From church in Old Basing turn **R** under railway bridge then after 1/2 mile, towards end of Old Basing, turn **R** by triangle of grass onto Newnham Lane 'Newnham'.

2 Easy to miss: after 2 1/2 miles, at X-roads (your priority) by telephone box in Newnham, turn **L** onto Ridge Lane 'Tylney Hall'.

3 After 3 1/2 miles, at start of Hartley Wespall village and immediately after bus shelter on left, turn **R** 'Turgis Green'.

4 At T-j with long red-brick wall to left, turn **R** 'Mattingley' then after almost 1/2 mile first **L** 'Daneshill School, Goodyears Green'.

5 At X-roads with busy A33 by Wellington Arms **SA** 'Stratfield Saye 1 3/4'.

6 Shortly after crossing bridge over River Loddon, on sharp right-hand bend, first **L** 'Stratfield Saye, Bramley' then at X-roads in Stratfield Saye by New Inn turn **L** 'Bramley'.

7 At X-roads go **SA** following signs for Bramley Station.

8 At T-j at end of Bramley Lane turn **R** over railway crossing 'Sherborne St John 3 1/2, Basingstoke 7'.

27 At next X-roads / traffic lights **SA** onto Milkingpen Lane 'Newnham' then shortly at T-j / X-roads turn **L** onto Church Lane. At church, dismount and walk through churchyard to return to start.

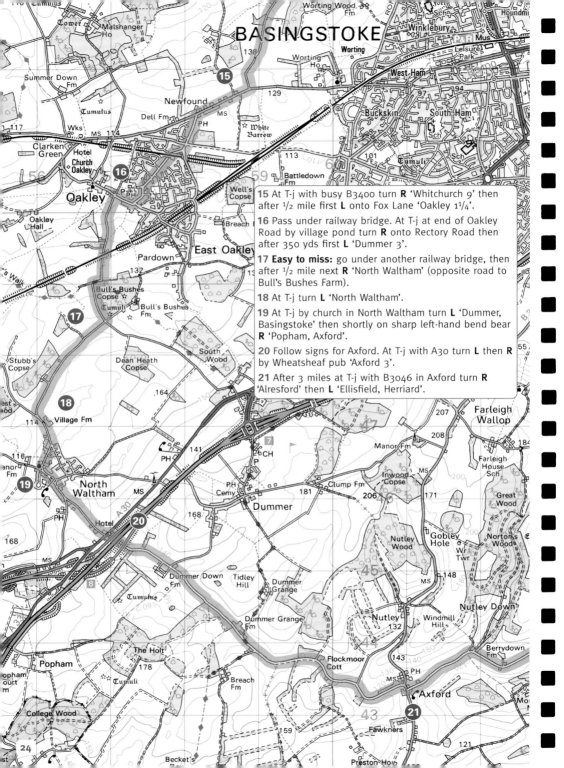

15 At T-j with busy B3400 turn **R** 'Whitchurch 9' then after ½ mile first **L** onto Fox Lane 'Oakley 1¼'.

16 Pass under railway bridge. At T-j at end of Oakley Road by village pond turn **R** onto Rectory Road then after 350 yds first **L** 'Dummer 3'.

17 Easy to miss: go under another railway bridge, then after ½ mile next **R** 'North Waltham' (opposite road to Bull's Bushes Farm).

18 At T-j turn **L** 'North Waltham'.

19 At T-j by church in North Waltham turn **L** 'Dummer, Basingstoke' then shortly on sharp left-hand bend bear **R** 'Popham, Axford'.

20 Follow signs for Axford. At T-j with A30 turn **L** then **R** by Wheatsheaf pub 'Axford 3'.

21 After 3 miles at T-j with B3046 in Axford turn **R** 'Alresford' then **L** 'Ellisfield, Herriard'.

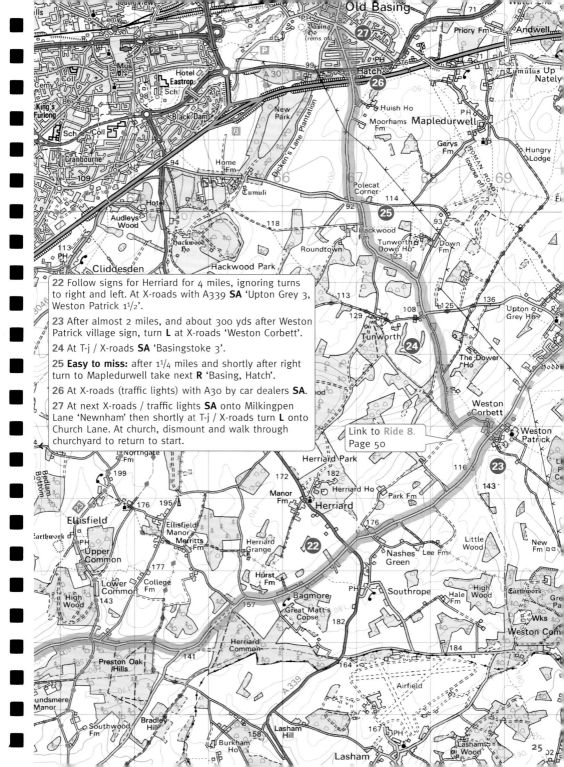

22 Follow signs for Herriard for 4 miles, ignoring turns to right and left. At X-roads with A339 **SA** 'Upton Grey 3, Weston Patrick 1 1/2'.

23 After almost 2 miles, and about 300 yds after Weston Patrick village sign, turn **L** at X-roads 'Weston Corbett'.

24 At T-j / X-roads **SA** 'Basingstoke 3'.

25 **Easy to miss:** after 1 1/4 miles and shortly after right turn to Mapledurwell take next **R** 'Basing, Hatch'.

26 At X-roads (traffic lights) with A30 by car dealers **SA**.

27 At next X-roads / traffic lights **SA** onto Milkingpen Lane 'Newnham' then shortly at T-j / X-roads turn **L** onto Church Lane. At church, dismount and walk through churchyard to return to start.

Link to Ride 8. Page 50

A ring around Andover from Whitchurch

There are times when maps throw up a whole series of unusual names that could easily fit into some Victorian melodrama. On this ride one could imagine Penton Mewsey and Penton Grafton set against the brothers Barton Stacey and Newton Stacey. The ruffians Monxton and Thruxton are up to no good and have already caused mayhem with poor Ragged Appleshaw until the issue is resolved by the local magistrate, Goodworth Clatford. Back in the real world this is an easy ride through the gently undulating countryside surrounding Andover, with clear-flowing chalk streams, big arable fields and a series of attractive villages, many boasting a fine array of thatched cottages, particularly in Amport. Between Amport and Monxton you may wish to divert less than a mile off the route to visit the Hawk Conservancy. More than 200 birds of prey can be seen in the 15 acres of woodland gardens, including bald eagles, peregrine falcons and the largest of all, the Andean condor. There are flying displays and feeding sessions. For more details go to www.hawk-conservancy. org. As you can see from the list of refreshments, there is no shortage of pubs along the way and there is also the welcome option of hot drinks and cakes at the post office in Abbotts Ann. Now how does she fit into the story?

Overview

On-road ● 32 miles / 52 kilometres ● Easy

Start
Roundabout in the centre of Whitchurch, off the A34 south of Newbury

Parking
Follow signs for free car park in centre of Whitchurch

Busy road
Almost ½ mile on A3057 between Fullerton and West Down to cross the River Test 16

Off-road sections
None

Terrain
Gently undulating with many short climbs of 100-200ft (30-60m) but no major hills

Nearest railway
Whitchurch

Refreshments
Whitchurch
Lots of choice

St Mary Bourne
George Inn
T: 01264 738340
Bourne Valley Inn
T: 01264 738361

Penton Mewsey
White Hart Inn
T: 01264 772236

Thruxton
White Horse PH
T: 01267 772401

Monxton
Black Swan PH
T: 01264 710260

Abbotts Ann
Eagle Inn
T: 01264 710339

Chilbolton
Abbots Mitre PH
T: 01264 860348

Barton Stacey
Swan Inn
T: 01962 760470

Other rides nearby

Ride 2 Page 14
Ride 4
Ride 5 Page 32

Map pages

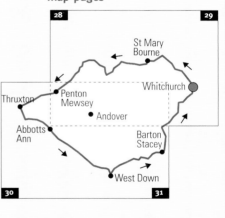

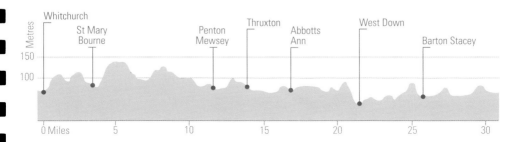

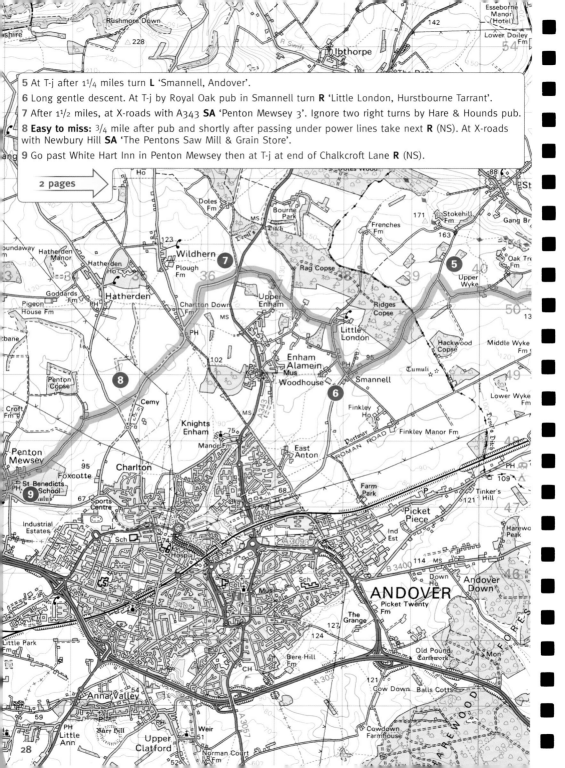

5 At T-j after 1¼ miles turn **L** 'Smannell, Andover'.

6 Long gentle descent. At T-j by Royal Oak pub in Smannell turn **R** 'Little London, Hurstbourne Tarrant'.

7 After 1½ miles, at X-roads with A343 **SA** 'Penton Mewsey 3'. Ignore two right turns by Hare & Hounds pub.

8 **Easy to miss:** ¾ mile after pub and shortly after passing under power lines take next **R** (NS). At X-roads with Newbury Hill **SA** 'The Pentons Saw Mill & Grain Store'.

9 Go past White Hart Inn in Penton Mewsey then at T-j at end of Chalkcroft Lane **R** (NS).

2 pages ➡

28

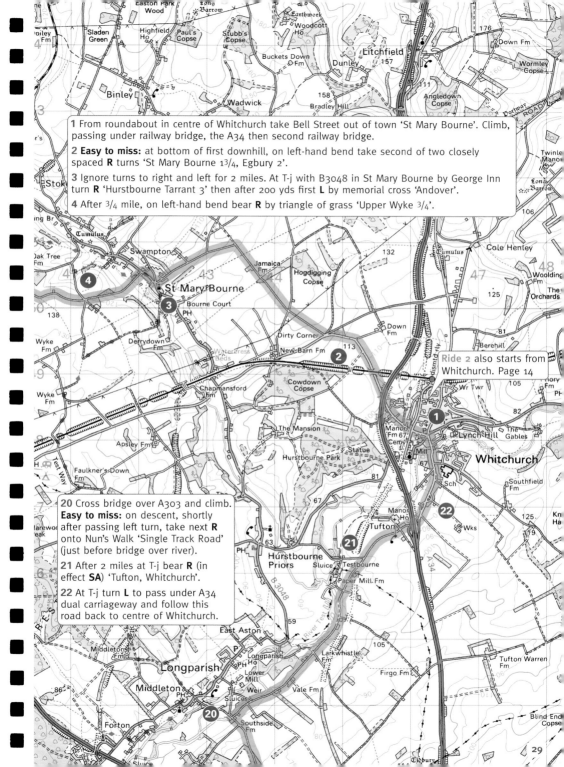

1 From roundabout in centre of Whitchurch take Bell Street out of town 'St Mary Bourne'. Climb, passing under railway bridge, the A34 then second railway bridge.

2 Easy to miss: at bottom of first downhill, on left-hand bend take second of two closely spaced **R** turns 'St Mary Bourne 1³/₄, Egbury 2'.

3 Ignore turns to right and left for 2 miles. At T-j with B3048 in St Mary Bourne by George Inn turn **R** 'Hurstbourne Tarrant 3' then after 200 yds first **L** by memorial cross 'Andover'.

4 After ³/₄ mile, on left-hand bend bear **R** by triangle of grass 'Upper Wyke ³/₄'.

Ride 2 also starts from Whitchurch. Page 14

20 Cross bridge over A303 and climb. **Easy to miss:** on descent, shortly after passing left turn, take next **R** onto Nun's Walk 'Single Track Road' (just before bridge over river).

21 After 2 miles at T-j bear **R** (in effect **SA**) 'Tufton, Whitchurch'.

22 At T-j turn **L** to pass under A34 dual carriageway and follow this road back to centre of Whitchurch.

29

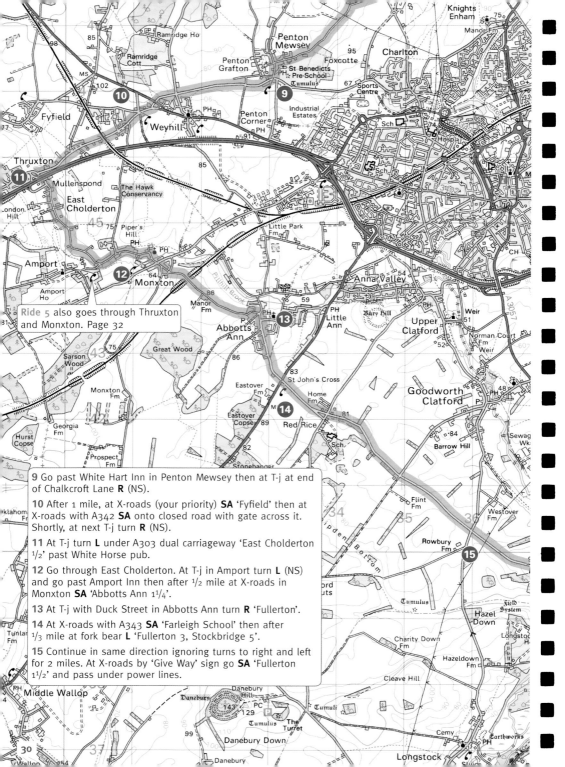

Ride 5 also goes through Thruxton and Monxton. Page 32

9 Go past White Hart Inn in Penton Mewsey then at T-j at end of Chalkcroft Lane **R** (NS).

10 After 1 mile, at X-roads (your priority) **SA** 'Fyfield' then at X-roads with A342 **SA** onto closed road with gate across it. Shortly, at next T-j turn **R** (NS).

11 At T-j turn **L** under A303 dual carriageway 'East Cholderton ¹/₂' past White Horse pub.

12 Go through East Cholderton. At T-j in Amport turn **L** (NS) and go past Amport Inn then after ¹/₂ mile at X-roads in Monxton **SA** 'Abbotts Ann 1¹/₄'.

13 At T-j with Duck Street in Abbotts Ann turn **R** 'Fullerton'.

14 At X-roads with A343 **SA** 'Farleigh School' then after ¹/₃ mile at fork bear **L** 'Fullerton 3, Stockbridge 5'.

15 Continue in same direction ignoring turns to right and left for 2 miles. At X-roads by 'Give Way' sign go **SA** 'Fullerton 1¹/₂' and pass under power lines.

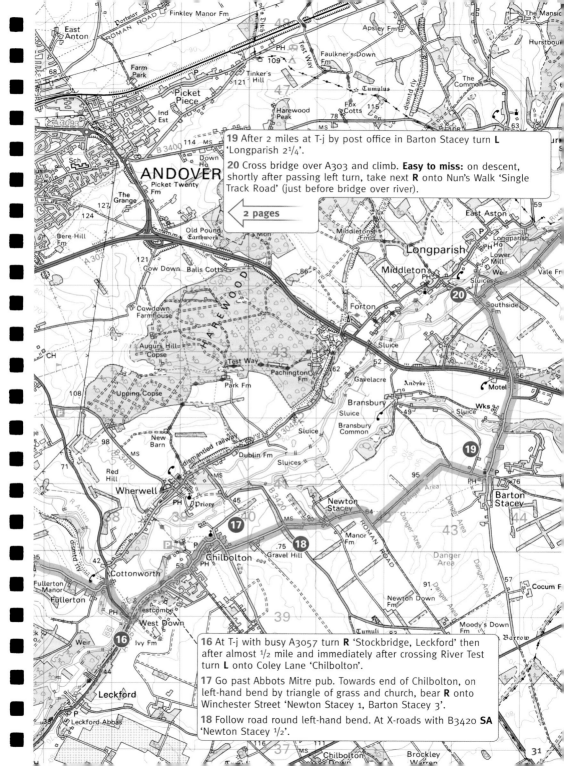

19 After 2 miles at T-j by post office in Barton Stacey turn **L** 'Longparish 2¼'.

20 Cross bridge over A303 and climb. **Easy to miss:** on descent, shortly after passing left turn, take next **R** onto Nun's Walk 'Single Track Road' (just before bridge over river).

2 pages

16 At T-j with busy A3057 turn **R** 'Stockbridge, Leckford' then after almost ½ mile and immediately after crossing River Test turn **L** onto Coley Lane 'Chilbolton'.

17 Go past Abbots Mitre pub. Towards end of Chilbolton, on left-hand bend by triangle of grass and church, bear **R** onto Winchester Street 'Newton Stacey 1, Barton Stacey 3'.

18 Follow road round left-hand bend. At X-roads with B3420 **SA** 'Newton Stacey ½'.

31

Stockbridge, Thruxton & the Wallops

Stockbridge has a fine, wide main street with lots of interesting shops, cafés and pubs on each side. It is a centre for fly fishing with people paying a fortune to spend a day trying their luck in the crystal-clear waters of the River Test, one of the most famous fishing rivers in the country. The town grew in importance when Welsh drovers rested there with their flocks on their way to various sheep fairs and markets in the Southeast. A thatched cottage known as 'Drovers House' has the message in Welsh painted on the wall: 'Seasoned hay, tasty pastures, good beer, comfortable beds'. After crossing the River Test and leaving Stockbridge, the ride soon passes Danebury, an Iron Age hill fort dating back 2,500 years. The area was a focal point for religious gatherings. There are plenty of thatched houses bedecked with flowers in the series of small villages through which the ride passes, namely Monxton, Amport, Thruxton and Grateley. Between Monxton and Amport you pass close to the Hawk Conservancy: for more details see the previous ride or go to www.hawk-conservancy.org. The shallow valley of Wallop Brook is followed through the villages of Over Wallop, Middle Wallop, Nether Wallop and Broughton to its junction with the River Test. Time to turn north and choose a tea shop in Stockbridge.

Overview

On-road ● 28 miles / 45 kilometres ● Easy

Start
Stockbridge, on the A30
northwest of Winchester

Parking
In the wide main street
of Stockbridge

Busy roads
About 200yds on the A343
beyond Danebury Hill Fort ❸

Off-road sections
None

Terrain
Gently undulating with several
short climbs of 100-200ft
(30-60m) but no major hills

Nearest railway
Grateley

Refreshments
Stockbridge
Lots of choice

Monxton
Black Swan PH
T: 01264 710260

Amport
Amport Inn
T: 01264 710371

Thruxton
George Inn
T: 01264 772480

Grateley
Plough Inn
T: 01264 889221

Over Wallop
White Hart PH
T: 01264 781331

Middle Wallop
George Inn
T: 01264 781224

Nether Wallop
Five Bells PH
T: 01264 781572

Broughton
Greyhound PH
T: 01794 301464
Tally Ho Inn
T: 01794 301280

Other rides nearby

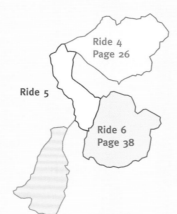

Ride 4
Page 26

Ride 5

Ride 6
Page 38

Ride 7
Page 44

Map pages

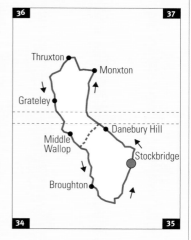

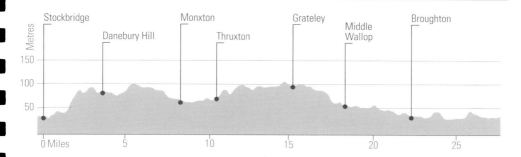

10 After 1³/4 miles at T-j with B3084 by memorial cross in Over Wallop turn **L** (NS). After ¹/2 mile at X-roads with A343 by George Inn **SA** onto Farley Street 'Nether Wallop'.

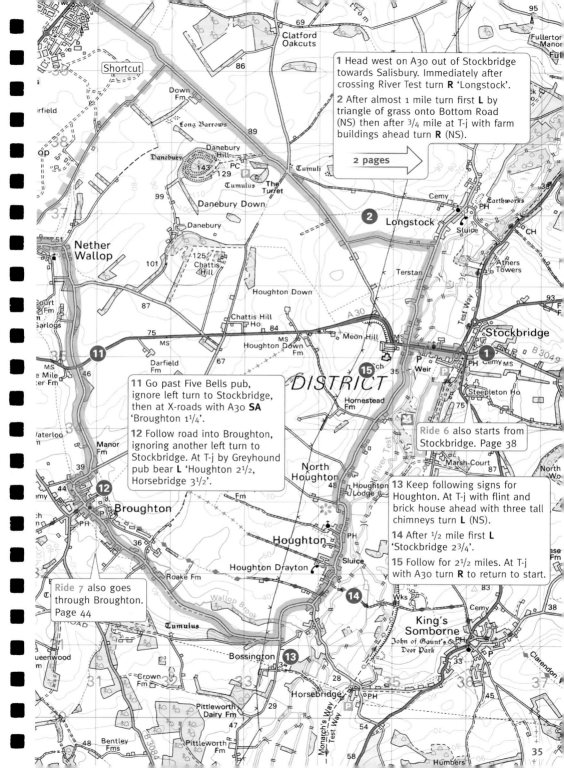

1 Head west on A30 out of Stockbridge towards Salisbury. Immediately after crossing River Test turn **R** 'Longstock'.

2 After almost 1 mile turn first **L** by triangle of grass onto Bottom Road (NS) then after 3/4 mile at T-j with farm buildings ahead turn **R** (NS).

2 pages →

11 Go past Five Bells pub, ignore left turn to Stockbridge, then at X-roads with A30 **SA** 'Broughton 1¹/4'.

12 Follow road into Broughton, ignoring another left turn to Stockbridge. At T-j by Greyhound pub bear **L** 'Houghton 2¹/2, Horsebridge 3¹/2'.

Ride 6 also starts from Stockbridge. Page 38

13 Keep following signs for Houghton. At T-j with flint and brick house ahead with three tall chimneys turn **L** (NS).

14 After ¹/2 mile first **L** 'Stockbridge 2³/4'.

15 Follow for 2¹/2 miles. At T-j with A30 turn **R** to return to start.

Ride 7 also goes through Broughton. Page 44

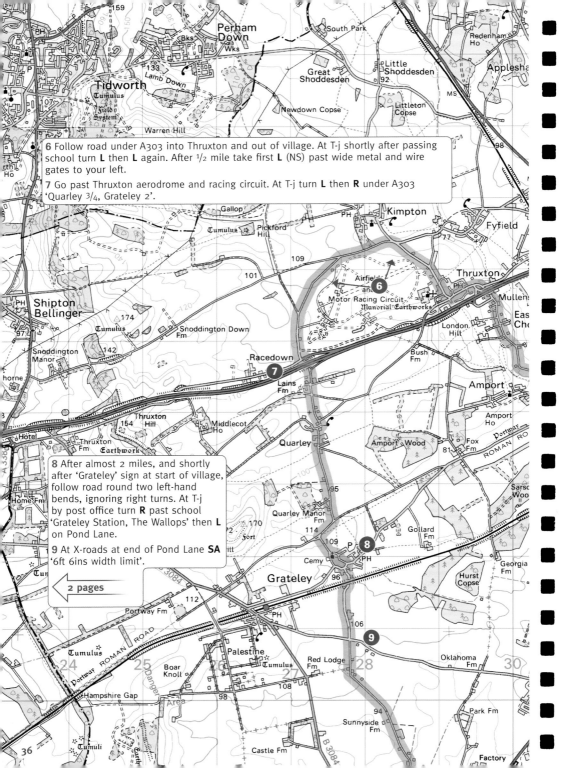

6 Follow road under A303 into Thruxton and out of village. At T-j shortly after passing school turn **L** then **L** again. After 1/2 mile take first **L** (NS) past wide metal and wire gates to your left.

7 Go past Thruxton aerodrome and racing circuit. At T-j turn **L** then **R** under A303 'Quarley 3/4, Grateley 2'.

8 After almost 2 miles, and shortly after 'Grateley' sign at start of village, follow road round two left-hand bends, ignoring right turns. At T-j by post office turn **R** past school 'Grateley Station, The Wallops' then **L** on Pond Lane.

9 At X-roads at end of Pond Lane **SA** '6ft 6ins width limit'.

2 pages

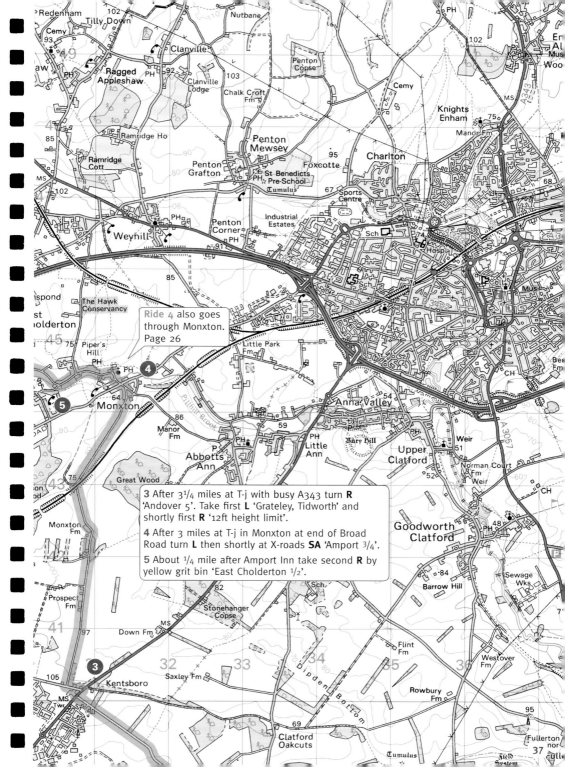

Ride 4 also goes through Monxton.
Page 26

3 After 3¼ miles at T-j with busy A343 turn **R** 'Andover 5'. Take first **L** 'Grateley, Tidworth' and shortly first **R** '12ft height limit'.

4 After 3 miles at T-j in Monxton at end of Broad Road turn **L** then shortly at X-roads **SA** 'Amport ¾'.

5 About ¼ mile after Amport Inn take second **R** by yellow grit bin 'East Cholderton ½'.

Stockbridge & the Test Valley

F ollow the sparkling waters of the River Test, one of the country's most famous fly-fishing rivers, south from Stockbridge through Houghton as far as Mottisfont. Owned by the openings of the grounds to allow visitors to enjoy the wonderful fragrance of the flowers, at its best later in the day. For those with a hunger and a thirst there is also a tearoom at the abbey! After but luckily there is a railway path that can be used for a mile before rejoining the lane network near Longstock. Be aware that, although it has a stone base, the railway path can get muddy in winter and

National Trust, Mottisfont Abbey was originally a 13th century priory and is set in landscaped grounds with ancient trees, walled gardens and the magnificent National Collection of Old Fashioned Roses with over 300 varieties. The roses are at their best in June and there are evening the almost flat run down to here there are a series of climbs in the middle part of the ride as it crosses the undulating downland to the west of Winchester. The final highpoint is reached just north of the A30 before a long descent to Leckford. The A3057 is a very busy road after prolonged rain. The traffic-free Test Way continues south from Stockbridge along the course of the old railway. It starts from the roundabout at the eastern edge of the town and is suitable for young children.

Overview

On-road ● 30 miles / 48 kilometres ● Easy / Moderate

Start
Stockbridge on the A30
northwest of Winchester

Parking
In the wide main street

Busy roads
● ¼ mile on A3057 east
of Mottisfont ❸

● ¼ mile on B3049
southwest of Crawley ⓫

Off-road sections
1 mile on railway path north of
Stockbridge (muddy after rain)
⓭ to ⓮

Terrain
The Test Valley is generally
flat, the downlands to the
east are undulating. Three
climbs over 200ft (60m)

Nearest railway
Dunbridge (near Mottisfont)

Refreshments
Stockbridge
Lots of choice

Houghton
Boot Inn
T: 01794 388310

Mottisfont Abbey Café
Open March to October
(not Fridays)
T: 01794 341220

Braishfield
Newport Inn
T: 01794 368225
Wheatsheaf PH
T: 01794 368372

Sparsholt
Plough PH
T: 01962 776353

Crawley
Fox & Hounds PH
T: 01962 776006

Longstock
Peat Spade Inn
T: 01264 810612

Other rides nearby

Ride 5
Page 32

Ride 6

Map pages

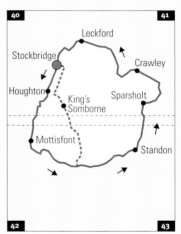

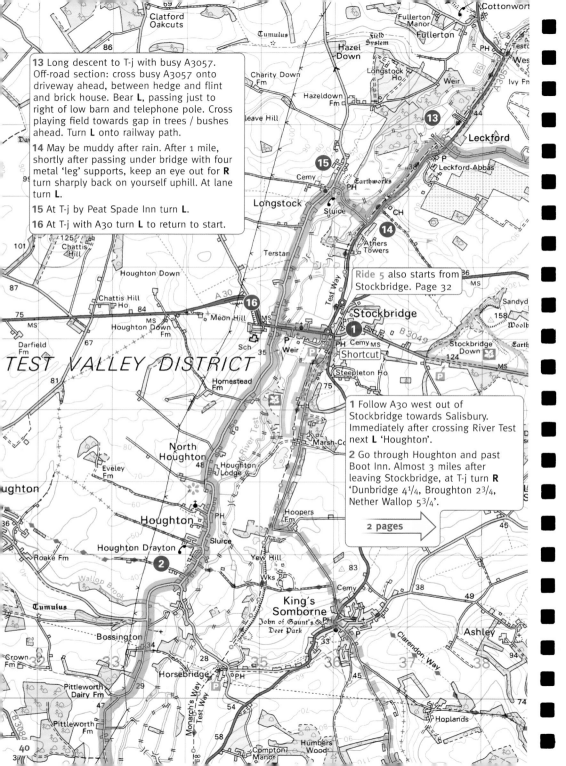

13 Long descent to T-j with busy A3057. Off-road section: cross busy A3057 onto driveway ahead, between hedge and flint and brick house. Bear **L**, passing just to right of low barn and telephone pole. Cross playing field towards gap in trees / bushes ahead. Turn **L** onto railway path.

14 May be muddy after rain. After 1 mile, shortly after passing under bridge with four metal 'leg' supports, keep an eye out for **R** turn sharply back on yourself uphill. At lane turn **L**.

15 At T-j by Peat Spade Inn turn **L**.

16 At T-j with A30 turn **L** to return to start.

Ride 5 also starts from Stockbridge. Page 32

1 Follow A30 west out of Stockbridge towards Salisbury. Immediately after crossing River Test next **L** 'Houghton'.

2 Go through Houghton and past Boot Inn. Almost 3 miles after leaving Stockbridge, at T-j turn **R** 'Dunbridge 4¼, Broughton 2¾, Nether Wallop 5¾'.

2 pages ➡

TEST VALLEY DISTRICT

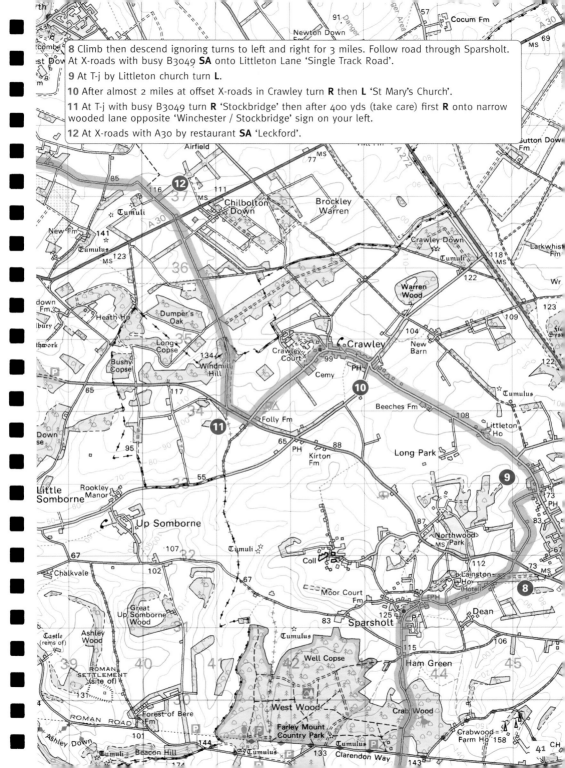

8 Climb then descend ignoring turns to left and right for 3 miles. Follow road through Sparsholt. At X-roads with busy B3049 **SA** onto Littleton Lane 'Single Track Road'.

9 At T-j by Littleton church turn **L**.

10 After almost 2 miles at offset X-roads in Crawley turn **R** then **L** 'St Mary's Church'.

11 At T-j with busy B3049 turn **R** 'Stockbridge' then after 400 yds (take care) first **R** onto narrow wooded lane opposite 'Winchester / Stockbridge' sign on your left.

12 At X-roads with A30 by restaurant **SA** 'Leckford'.

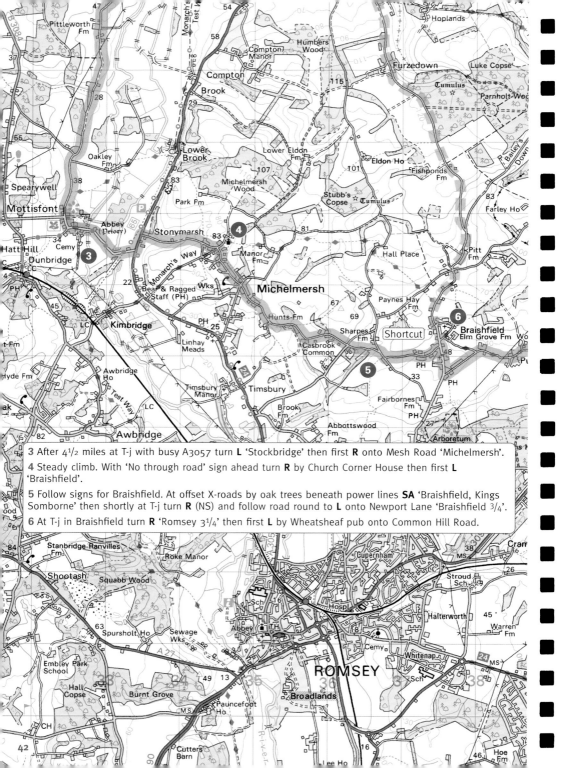

3 After 4½ miles at T-j with busy A3057 turn **L** 'Stockbridge' then first **R** onto Mesh Road 'Michelmersh'.

4 Steady climb. With 'No through road' sign ahead turn **R** by Church Corner House then first **L** 'Braishfield'.

5 Follow signs for Braishfield. At offset X-roads by oak trees beneath power lines **SA** 'Braishfield, Kings Somborne' then shortly at T-j turn **R** (NS) and follow road round to **L** onto Newport Lane 'Braishfield ¾'.

6 At T-j in Braishfield turn **R** 'Romsey 3¼' then first **L** by Wheatsheaf pub onto Common Hill Road.

7 Over next 4 miles climb then descend. At T-j with A3090 turn **L** 'Winchester 4' then shortly **L** again 'Farley Mount 2¾, Sparsholt 3'.

2 pages

From Broughton to the edge of the New Forest

The New Forest is best explored by bike via its off-road tracks (see off-road Ride 4, page 110) as the roads that run across it, almost without exception, carry quite high levels of traffic. It is also worth visiting the National Park website at www.new-forest-national-park.com and following links to 'Cycling' for downloadable maps. This ride just touches on the northern edge of the New Forest giving you the opportunity of seeing the wonderful broadleaf woodland, wild ponies and perhaps deer, which abound in the area. The ride starts from Broughton, a pretty village to the southwest of Stockbridge, and runs south, parallel to the Test Valley. After crossing the A36 in West Wellow, a short section of broad stone-based track neatly links quiet lanes and avoids spending time on busy roads. You are now within the boundaries of the New Forest as far as Nomansland

and should glimpse plenty of wildlife. The section between Hamptworth and the A36 at Newton is the busiest of the ride for reasons hard to fathom. North of here you climb to a highpoint of 480ft (146m) on Dean Hill. Having briefly strayed into Wiltshire you return to Hampshire in West Dean with one final

climb on your way back to Broughton. The Test Valley lies just to the east of Broughton and it would be very easy to link this ride via the lanes alongside the river to either of the two rides from Stockbridge for a longer day out.

Overview
On-road ● 32 miles / 52 kilometres ● Easy / Moderate

Start
Broughton, off the A30 south
of Andover and southwest of
Stockbridge

Parking
At the back of Broughton
village hall, on the road
towards Houghton

Busy roads
1/4 mile on A27 through
Whiteparish (30mph speed
limit) **16**

Off-road sections
About 1/4 mile on a wide stone
track south of the A36 at West
Wellow **10**

Terrain
Undulating with several climbs
of 100-200ft (30-60m) and
three longer climbs

Nearest railway
Dundridge, northeast
of Romsey

Refreshments
Broughton
Lots of choice

East Tytherley
Star Inn
T: 01794 340225

Lockerley
Kings Arms PH
T: 01794 340332

Canada
Rockingham Arms PH
T: 01794 322473

Nomansland
Lamb Inn
T: 01794 390246

Hamptworth
Cuckoo Inn
T: 01794 390302

Whiteparish
Fountain Inn
T: 01794 884266
Kings Head PH
T: 01794 884287

West Tytherley
Black Horse PH
T: 01794 340308

Other rides nearby

Ride 5
Page 32

Ride 7

Map pages

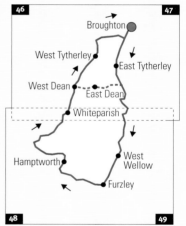

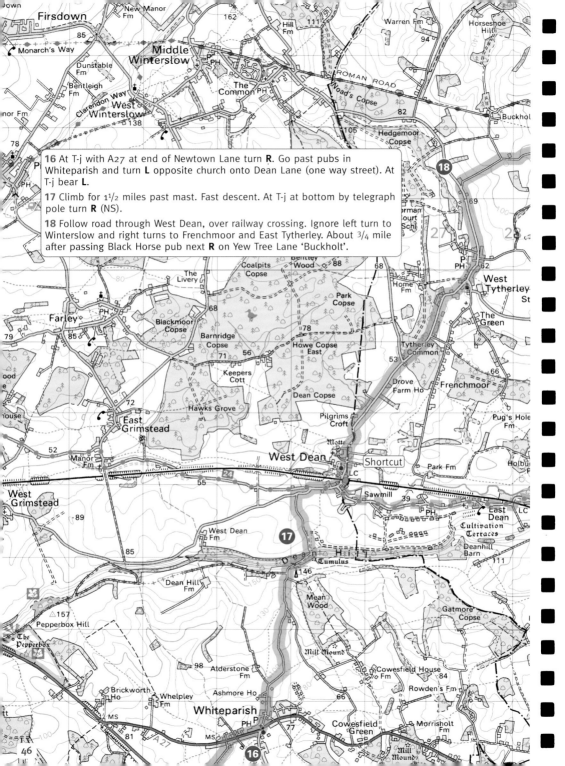

16 At T-j with A27 at end of Newtown Lane turn **R**. Go past pubs in Whiteparish and turn **L** opposite church onto Dean Lane (one way street). At T-j bear **L**.

17 Climb for 1½ miles past mast. Fast descent. At T-j at bottom by telegraph pole turn **R** (NS).

18 Follow road through West Dean, over railway crossing. Ignore left turn to Winterslow and right turns to Frenchmoor and East Tytherley. About ¾ mile after passing Black Horse pub next **R** on Yew Tree Lane 'Buckholt'.

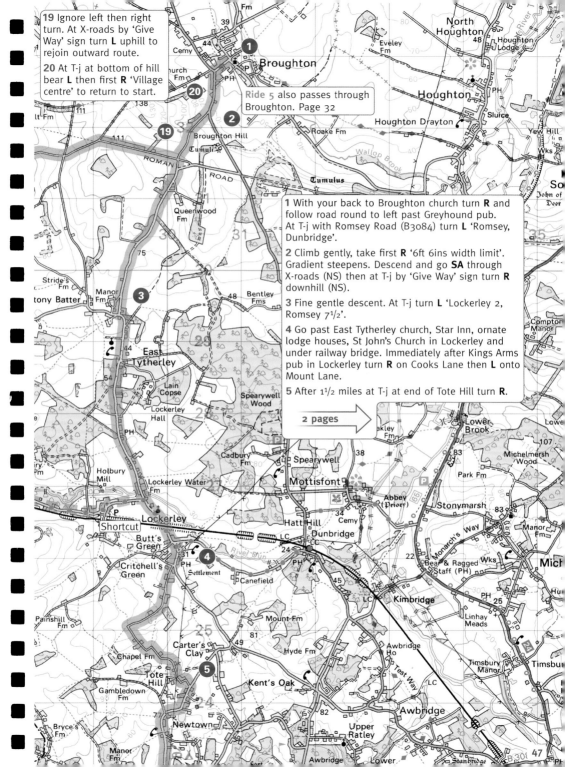

19 Ignore left then right turn. At X-roads by 'Give Way' sign turn **L** uphill to rejoin outward route.

20 At T-j at bottom of hill bear **L** then first **R** 'Village centre' to return to start.

Ride 5 also passes through Broughton. Page 32

1 With your back to Broughton church turn **R** and follow road round to left past Greyhound pub.
At T-j with Romsey Road (B3084) turn **L** 'Romsey, Dunbridge'.

2 Climb gently, take first **R** '6ft 6ins width limit'. Gradient steepens. Descend and go **SA** through X-roads (NS) then at T-j by 'Give Way' sign turn **R** downhill (NS).

3 Fine gentle descent. At T-j turn **L** 'Lockerley 2, Romsey 7½'.

4 Go past East Tytherley church, Star Inn, ornate lodge houses, St John's Church in Lockerley and under railway bridge. Immediately after Kings Arms pub in Lockerley turn **R** on Cooks Lane then **L** onto Mount Lane.

5 After 1½ miles at T-j at end of Tote Hill turn **R**.

2 pages

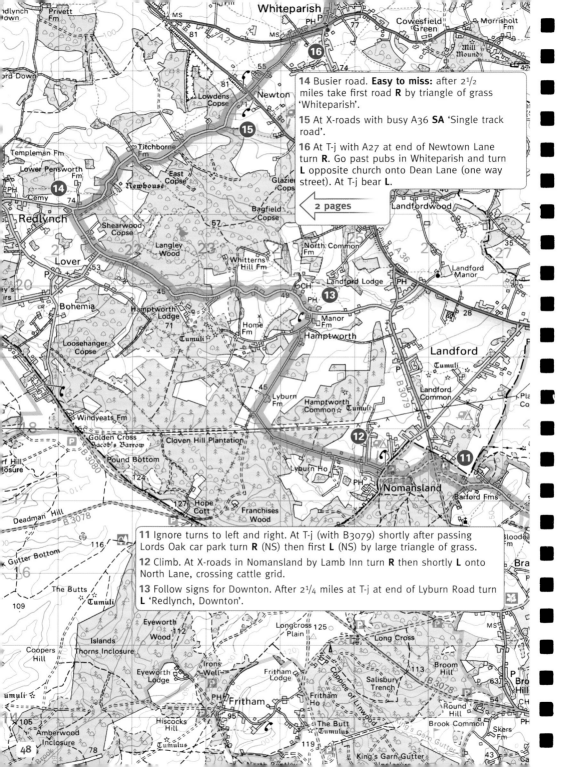

14 Busier road. **Easy to miss:** after 2½ miles take first road **R** by triangle of grass 'Whiteparish'.

15 At X-roads with busy A36 **SA** 'Single track road'.

16 At T-j with A27 at end of Newtown Lane turn **R**. Go past pubs in Whiteparish and turn **L** opposite church onto Dean Lane (one way street). At T-j bear **L**.

2 pages ◄

11 Ignore turns to left and right. At T-j (with B3079) shortly after passing Lords Oak car park turn **R** (NS) then first **L** (NS) by large triangle of grass.

12 Climb. At X-roads in Nomansland by Lamb Inn turn **R** then shortly **L** onto North Lane, crossing cattle grid.

13 Follow signs for Downton. After 2¼ miles at T-j at end of Lyburn Road turn **L** 'Redlynch, Downton'.

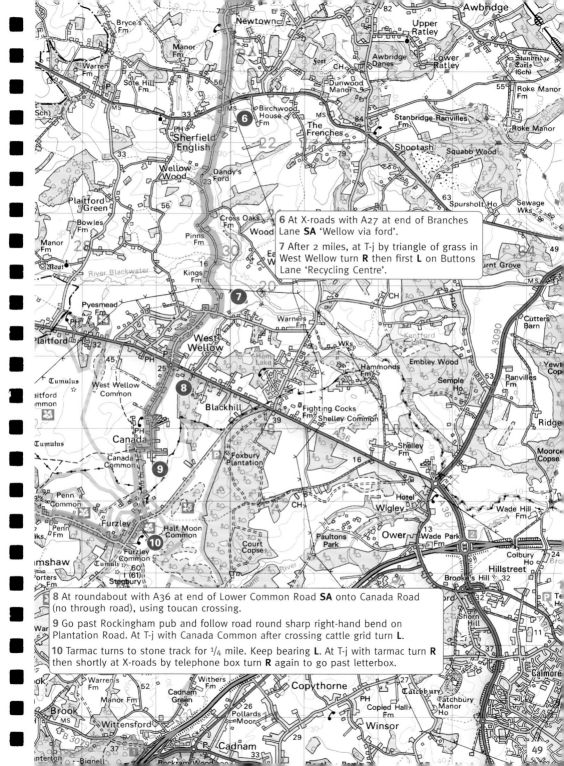

6 At X-roads with A27 at end of Branches Lane **SA** 'Wellow via ford'.

7 After 2 miles, at T-j by triangle of grass in West Wellow turn **R** then first **L** on Buttons Lane 'Recycling Centre'.

8 At roundabout with A36 at end of Lower Common Road **SA** onto Canada Road (no through road), using toucan crossing.

9 Go past Rockingham pub and follow road round sharp right-hand bend on Plantation Road. At T-j with Canada Common after crossing cattle grid turn **L**.

10 Tarmac turns to stone track for ¼ mile. Keep bearing **L**. At T-j with tarmac turn **R** then shortly at X-roads by telephone box turn **R** again to go past letterbox.

49

New Alresford to Odiham

Two rides start from New Alresford, one of the most attractive towns in Hampshire with its lime trees, wide streets, colour-washed Georgian buildings, good cafés and pubs. The ride starts from the car park of the Mid-Hants Railway, where restored steam trains run 10 miles up to Alton. It is called the Watercress Line as it was once used by growers to get produce to market. Leave town to the north, crossing the River Itchen at its exit from the lovely lake known as Old Alresford Pond. Before long you plunge into the network of tiny, quiet lanes that head northeast from Bighton through Lower Wield and Bradley to the

wider, rolling road heading east from Preston Candover towards Herriard and Upton Grey. Like New Alresford, Odiham is a handsome town with a wide main street and lots of old red-brick buildings – and a good choice of cafés and pubs. Many of the Georgian facades have been grafted onto earlier timber-

framed houses. The ride turns south past the RAF airfield and climbs to the highpoint of the ride between Long Sutton and Golden Pot, with the best views of the day. There are pubs in each of the villages as you continue southwest to rejoin the outward route in Bighton and drop back down to New Alresford.

Overview

On-road ● 38 miles / 61 kilometres ● Moderate

Start
New Alresford, off the A31 east of Winchester

Parking
Large car park by Watercress Line railway station (off the main street)

Busy roads
The B3046 at the start is the busiest road used ❶

Off-road sections
None

Terrain
Undulating with a few short climbs of 100-200ft (30-60m) and three longer ones

Nearest railway
Alton or Hook

Refreshments
New Alresford
Lots of choice

Lower Wield
Yew Tree PH (just off route)
T: 01256 389224

Upton Grey
Hoddington Arms PH
T: 01256 862371

Odiham
Lots of choice

Golden Pot
Golden Pot PH
T: 01420 80655

Bentworth
Star Inn
T: 01420 561224

Medstead
Castle of Comfort PH
T: 01420 562112

Bighton
Three Horseshoes PH
T: 01962 732859

Other rides nearby

Ride 3
Page 20

Ride 8

Ride 9
Page 56

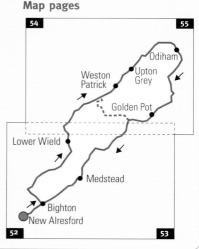

Map pages

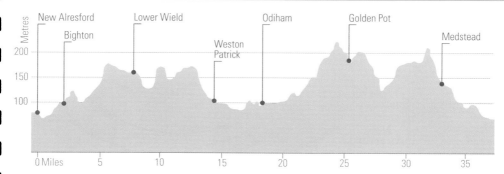

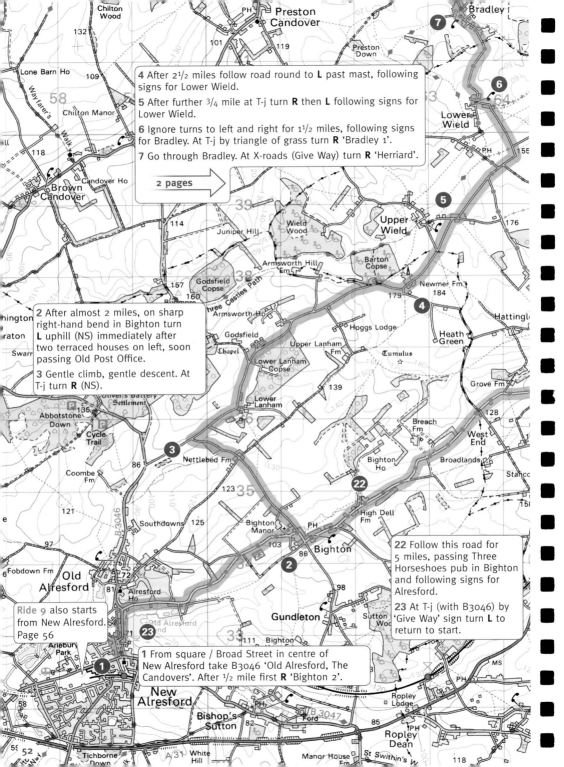

4 After 2½ miles follow road round to **L** past mast, following signs for Lower Wield.

5 After further ¾ mile at T-j turn **R** then **L** following signs for Lower Wield.

6 Ignore turns to left and right for 1½ miles, following signs for Bradley. At T-j by triangle of grass turn **R** 'Bradley 1'.

7 Go through Bradley. At X-roads (Give Way) turn **R** 'Herriard'.

2 pages ➡

2 After almost 2 miles, on sharp right-hand bend in Bighton turn **L** uphill (NS) immediately after two terraced houses on left, soon passing Old Post Office.

3 Gentle climb, gentle descent. At T-j turn **R** (NS).

22 Follow this road for 5 miles, passing Three Horseshoes pub in Bighton and following signs for Alresford.

23 At T-j (with B3046) by 'Give Way' sign turn **L** to return to start.

Ride 9 also starts from New Alresford. Page 56

1 From square / Broad Street in centre of New Alresford take B3046 'Old Alresford, The Candovers'. After ½ mile first **R** 'Bighton 2'.

52

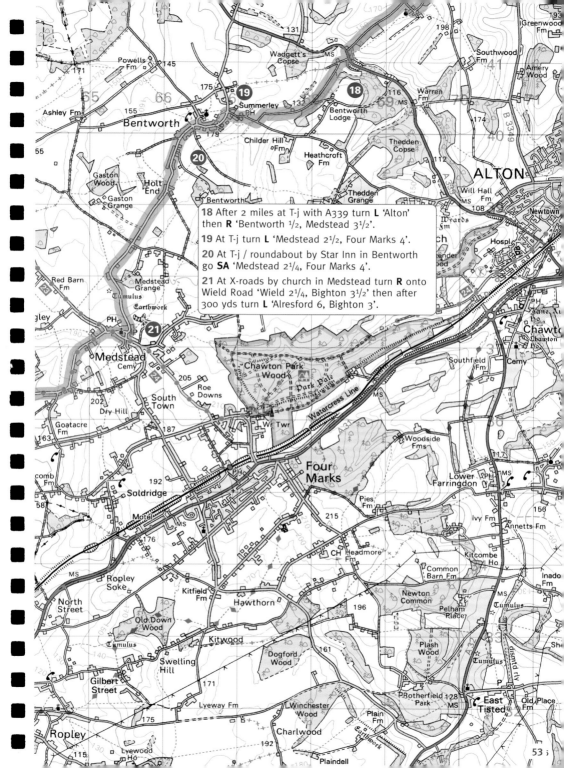

18 After 2 miles at T-j with A339 turn **L** 'Alton' then **R** 'Bentworth ¹/₂, Medstead 3¹/₂'.

19 At T-j turn **L** 'Medstead 2¹/₂, Four Marks 4'.

20 At T-j / roundabout by Star Inn in Bentworth go **SA** 'Medstead 2¹/₄, Four Marks 4'.

21 At X-roads by church in Medstead turn **R** onto Wield Road 'Wield 2¹/₄, Bighton 3¹/₂' then after 300 yds turn **L** 'Alresford 6, Bighton 3'.

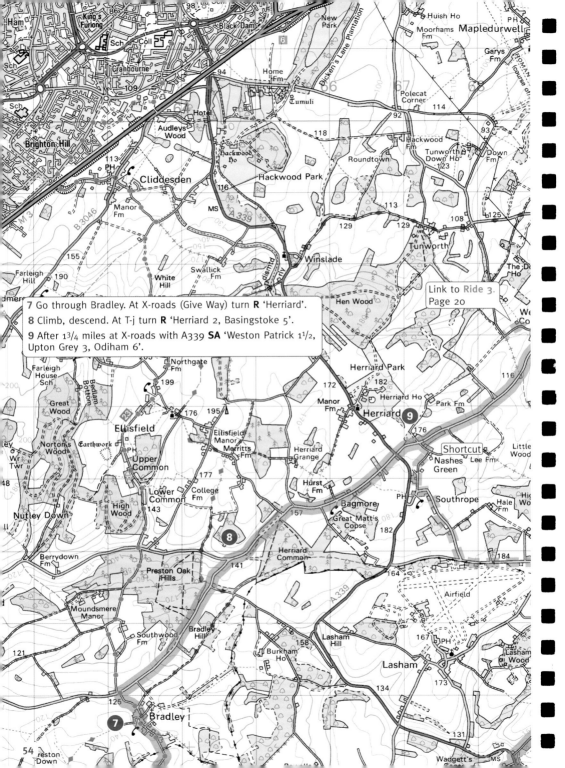

7 Go through Bradley. At X-roads (Give Way) turn **R** 'Herriard'.

8 Climb, descend. At T-j turn **R** 'Herriard 2, Basingstoke 5'.

9 After 1³/₄ miles at X-roads with A339 **SA** 'Weston Patrick 1¹/₂, Upton Grey 3, Odiham 6'.

Link to Ride 3. Page 20

Shortcut

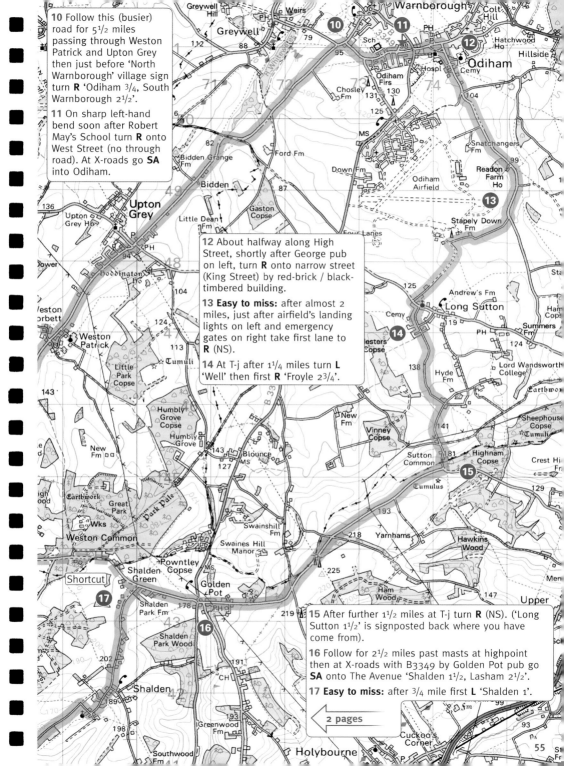

10 Follow this (busier) road for 5½ miles passing through Weston Patrick and Upton Grey then just before 'North Warnborough' village sign turn **R** 'Odiham 3/4, South Warnborough 2½'.

11 On sharp left-hand bend soon after Robert May's School turn **R** onto West Street (no through road). At X-roads go **SA** into Odiham.

12 About halfway along High Street, shortly after George pub on left, turn **R** onto narrow street (King Street) by red-brick / black-timbered building.

13 Easy to miss: after almost 2 miles, just after airfield's landing lights on left and emergency gates on right take first lane to **R** (NS).

14 At T-j after 1¼ miles turn **L** 'Well' then first **R** 'Froyle 2¾'.

15 After further 1½ miles at T-j turn **R** (NS). ('Long Sutton 1½' is signposted back where you have come from).

16 Follow for 2½ miles past masts at highpoint then at X-roads with B3349 by Golden Pot pub go **SA** onto The Avenue 'Shalden 1½, Lasham 2½'.

17 Easy to miss: after ¾ mile first **L** 'Shalden 1'.

Shortcut

2 pages

Above the Meon Valley south of New Alresford

The second of two rides starting from the handsome town of New Alresford, this one heads south from the centre of town to cross the bridge over the A31 and reach the pretty village of Cheriton. The ride really takes off soon after passing The Milbury's pub, at the top of a steady climb. Delightfully quiet wooded lanes run south from Lane End through Upham to the outskirts of Bishop's Waltham. If you are prepared to brave the traffic you may wish to visit the fine ruins of the Bishop of Winchester's Palace. It was built in 1135 but was largely destroyed in the Civil War in the 17th century. This is only an option, as the main route crosses the B3035 and continues on the wonderful network of lanes that climb to the highpoint on Beacon Hill, with splendid views east over the Meon Valley. Crafty choices of route enable you

to go straight across both the A272 and the A31, and thus avoid the dangers of trucks and vans. The route via Bighton provides the best entry back into New Alresford.

NB The A31, A272 and the B3047 east from New Alresford to the A31 near Ropley Dean are all very busy roads. The route described below to return to New Alresford may seem very circuitous but it provides safe crossings of the two A roads and avoids the B3047.

Overview
On-road ● 30 miles / 48 kilometres ● Moderate

Start
New Alresford, off the A31 east of Winchester

Parking
Large car park by Watercress Line railway station in New Alresford (off the main street)

Busy roads
The B3046 south out of New Alresford is the busiest road used **1** to **2**

NB Do not be tempted to return to the start along the B3047 from the A31 roundabout - it is very busy and not pleasant by bike

Off-road sections
None

Terrain
Undulating, with several climbs of 100-200ft (30-60m) and three longer ones

Nearest railway
Shawford (south of Winchester)

Refreshments
New Alresford
Lots of choice

Cheriton
Flower Pots Inn
T: 01962 771318

Upham
Brushmakers Arms PH
T: 01489 860231

Dundridge
Hampshire Bowman PH
T: 01489 892940

Bighton
Three Horseshoes PH
T: 01962 732859

Golden Pot
Golden Pot PH
T: 01420 80655

Bentworth
Star Inn
T: 01420 561224

Other rides nearby

Ride 8
Page 50

Ride 11
Page 68

Ride 9

Ride 12
Page 74

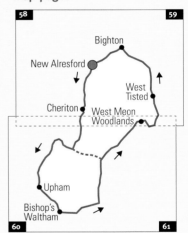

Map pages

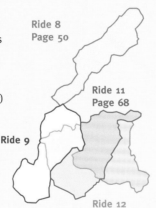

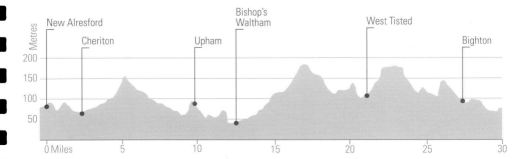

21 Follow this road through Bighton then after 2 miles, at T-j with B3046 turn **L** to return to start.

Ride 8 also starts from New Alresford. Page 50

1 From Watercress Line station car park in New Alresford follow signs for 'Overflow car park'. At T-j at end of Station Approach (with Methodist Church ahead) turn **L** under railway bridge.

2 Cross bridge over A31. After 2 miles, at end of Cheriton village, just after memorial cross and just before road crosses small stone bridge over stream, turn **R** 'Winchester 7, Bishop's Waltham 6'.

3 At X-roads with A272 **SA** 'Beauworth 3/4, Bishop's Waltham 6'.

2 pages →

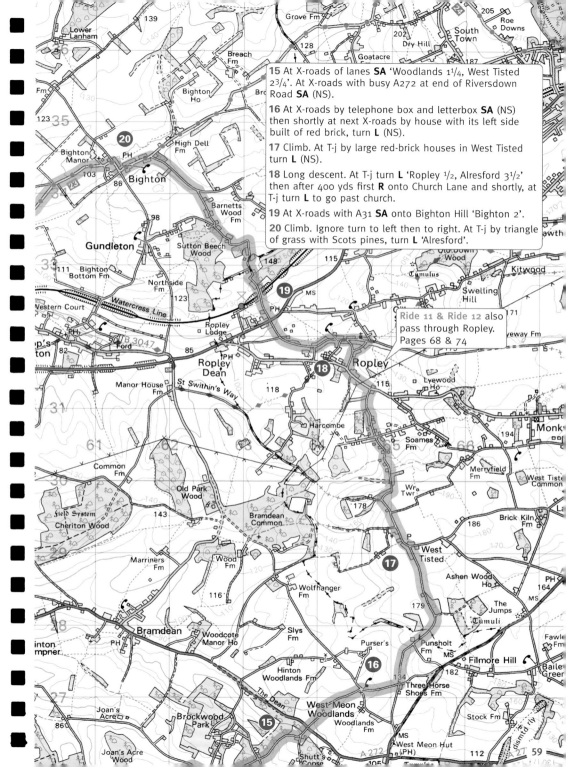

15 At X-roads of lanes **SA** 'Woodlands 1¼, West Tisted 2¾'. At X-roads with busy A272 at end of Riversdown Road **SA** (NS).

16 At X-roads by telephone box and letterbox **SA** (NS) then shortly at next X-roads by house with its left side built of red brick, turn **L** (NS).

17 Climb. At T-j by large red-brick houses in West Tisted turn **L** (NS).

18 Long descent. At T-j turn **L** 'Ropley ½, Alresford 3½' then after 400 yds first **R** onto Church Lane and shortly, at T-j turn **L** to go past church.

19 At X-roads with A31 **SA** onto Bighton Hill 'Bighton 2'.

20 Climb. Ignore turn to left then to right. At T-j by triangle of grass with Scots pines, turn **L** 'Alresford'.

Ride 11 & Ride 12 also pass through Ropley. Pages 68 & 74

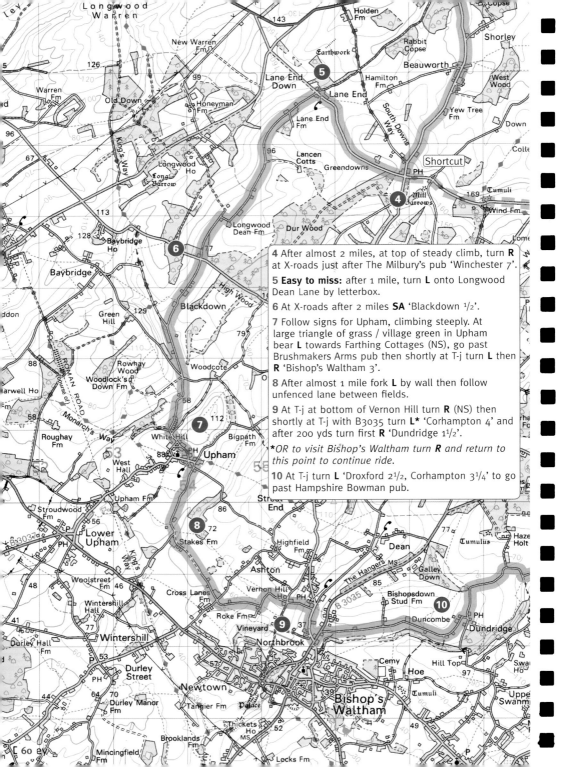

4 After almost 2 miles, at top of steady climb, turn **R** at X-roads just after The Milbury's pub 'Winchester 7'.

5 Easy to miss: after 1 mile, turn **L** onto Longwood Dean Lane by letterbox.

6 At X-roads after 2 miles **SA** 'Blackdown ½'.

7 Follow signs for Upham, climbing steeply. At large triangle of grass / village green in Upham bear **L** towards Farthing Cottages (NS), go past Brushmakers Arms pub then shortly at T-j turn **L** then **R** 'Bishop's Waltham 3'.

8 After almost 1 mile fork **L** by wall then follow unfenced lane between fields.

9 At T-j at bottom of Vernon Hill turn **R** (NS) then shortly at T-j with B3035 turn **L*** 'Corhampton 4' and after 200 yds turn first **R** 'Dundridge 1½'.

OR to visit Bishop's Waltham turn R and return to this point to continue ride.

10 At T-j turn **L** 'Droxford 2½, Corhampton 3¼' to go past Hampshire Bowman pub.

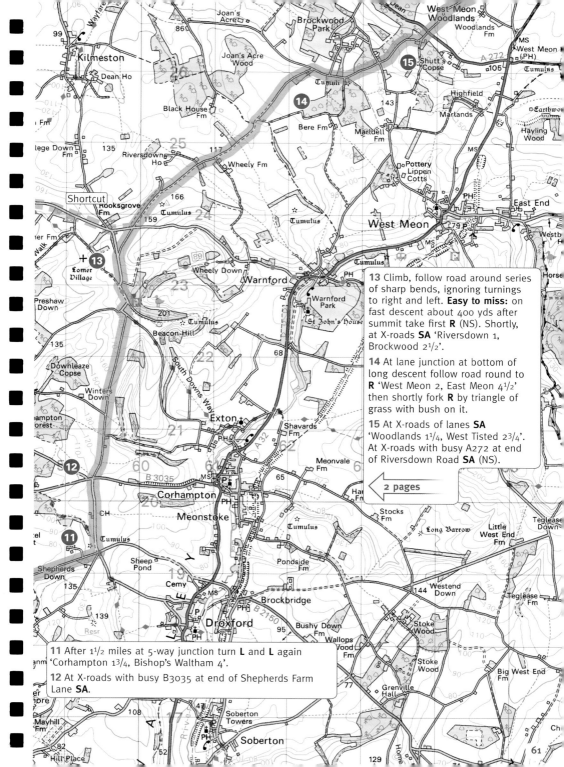

13 Climb, follow road around series of sharp bends, ignoring turnings to right and left. **Easy to miss:** on fast descent about 400 yds after summit take first **R** (NS). Shortly, at X-roads **SA** 'Riversdown 1, Brockwood 2½'.

14 At lane junction at bottom of long descent follow road round to **R** 'West Meon 2, East Meon 4½' then shortly fork **R** by triangle of grass with bush on it.

15 At X-roads of lanes **SA** 'Woodlands 1¼, West Tisted 2¾'. At X-roads with busy A272 at end of Riversdown Road **SA** (NS).

← 2 pages

11 After 1½ miles at 5-way junction turn **L** and **L** again 'Corhampton 1¾, Bishop's Waltham 4'.

12 At X-roads with busy B3035 at end of Shepherds Farm Lane **SA**.

61

East Meon north to Farringdon

East Meon is one of the finest bases in Hampshire for the lane cycling described in this book. In every direction there are wonderfully quiet roads through beautiful rolling scenery, and if the routes out of East Meon often start with a climb they also finish with a descent. The village has two pubs, stores, a free car park and a very fine church set against the backdrop of the steep grass slopes of Park Hill. This ride starts with two steep climbs in quick succession out of the Meon Valley north to the A272, then north again to cross the A32. This is definitely a ride (as with many others in the book) that is better second or third time round as you will spend the first time working out all the junctions that are inevitable in a quest to avoid busy roads. Instruction overload eases after recrossing the A32 between Lower and Upper Farringdon, the latter boasting an extraordinarily ornate red-brick village hall. Gawp at the amazing chalk cuttings either side of the road between West Worldham and Oakhanger, then turn south on lovely wooded lanes through Blackmoor and Hawkley. The climb that follows Hawkley is perhaps the steepest road climb in the book. Continue climbing more gently to the highpoint near Warren Corner. From here, with one short exception south of the A272, the course of the route is downwards back to the start in East Meon.

Overview

On-road ● 33 miles / 53 kilometres ● Moderate / Strenuous

Start
East Meon, off the A272
west of Petersfield

Parking
Follow signs for free car park
from Ye Olde George Inn

Busy roads
None

Off-road sections
None

Terrain
Undulating with several climbs
of 100-200ft (30-60m) and
three longer ones

Nearest railway
Alton or Liss

Refreshments
East Meon
Ye Olde George PH
T: 01730 823481
Izaak Walton PH
T: 01730 823252

Upper Farringdon
(400yds off route)
Rose & Crown PH
T: 01420 588231

Oakhanger
Red Lion PH
T: 01420 472232

Hawkley
Hawkley Inn
T: 01730 827205

Southwest of Hawkley
Trooper PH
T: 01730 827293

Other rides nearby

Ride 10

Ride 11
Page 68

Ride 12
Page 74

Ride 14
Page 86

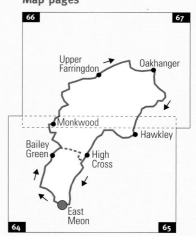

Map pages

66 · 67

Upper Farringdon — Oakhanger
Monkwood
Bailey Green · High Cross · Hawkley
East Meon

64 · 65

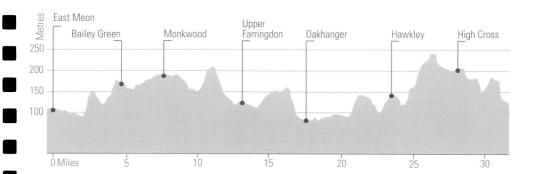

East Meon
Bailey Green
Monkwood
Upper Farringdon
Oakhanger
Hawkley
High Cross

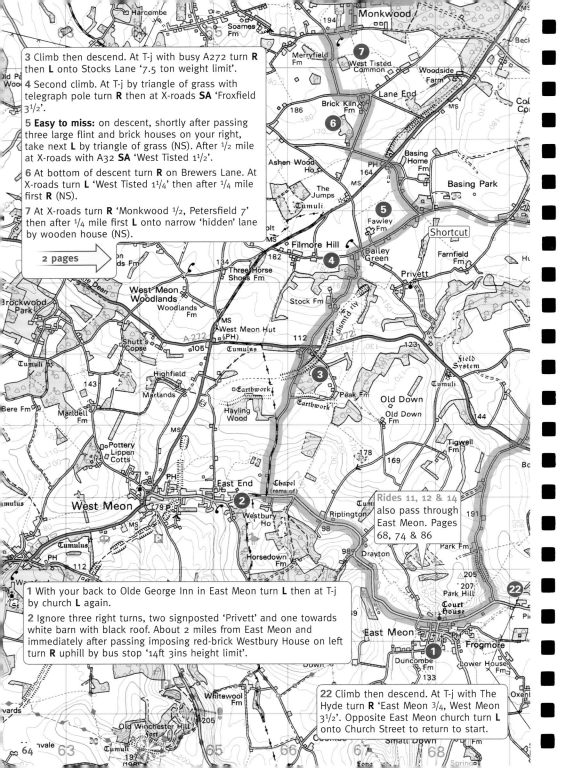

3 Climb then descend. At T-j with busy A272 turn **R** then **L** onto Stocks Lane '7.5 ton weight limit'.

4 Second climb. At T-j by triangle of grass with telegraph pole turn **R** then at X-roads **SA** 'Froxfield 3½'.

5 **Easy to miss:** on descent, shortly after passing three large flint and brick houses on your right, take next **L** by triangle of grass (NS). After ½ mile at X-roads with A32 **SA** 'West Tisted 1½'.

6 At bottom of descent turn **R** on Brewers Lane. At X-roads turn **L** 'West Tisted 1¼' then after ¼ mile first **R** (NS).

7 At X-roads turn **R** 'Monkwood ½, Petersfield 7' then after ¼ mile first **L** onto narrow 'hidden' lane by wooden house (NS).

2 pages →

Rides 11, 12 & 14 also pass through East Meon. Pages 68, 74 & 86

1 With your back to Olde George Inn in East Meon turn **L** then at T-j by church **L** again.

2 Ignore three right turns, two signposted 'Privett' and one towards white barn with black roof. About 2 miles from East Meon and immediately after passing imposing red-brick Westbury House on left turn **R** uphill by bus stop '14ft 3ins height limit'.

22 Climb then descend. At T-j with The Hyde turn **R** 'East Meon ¾, West Meon 3½'. Opposite East Meon church turn **L** onto Church Street to return to start.

18 Follow signs for Hawkley, ignoring left then right turn. Climb through lovely woodland. At T-j at top turn **L** 'Liss 2¼' then first **R** 'Priors Dean 1½'.

19 Follow road through Hawkley and signs for Priors Dean. Ignore left to Oakshott. Short, very steep climb then at triangle of grass by telephone box turn **L** 'Petersfield 5'.

20 Continue climbing. At T-j at top turn **L** 'Steep 2, Petersfield 3'.
Easy to miss: on descent, shortly after passing Trooper pub, next **R** 'Froxfield 1¼' then at X-roads turn **R** 'Froxfield 1, Privett 4'.

21 Ignore turnings to right and left, continuing **SA** at two X-roads (at second take road between two triangles of grass). At X-roads with busy A272 go **SA** (NS).

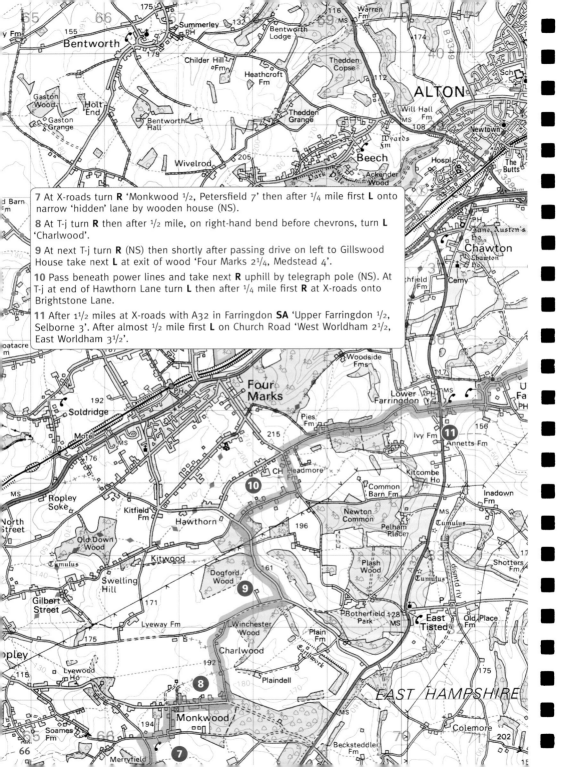

7 At X-roads turn **R** 'Monkwood ¹/₂, Petersfield 7' then after ¹/₄ mile first **L** onto narrow 'hidden' lane by wooden house (NS).

8 At T-j turn **R** then after ¹/₂ mile, on right-hand bend before chevrons, turn **L** 'Charlwood'.

9 At next T-j turn **R** (NS) then shortly after passing drive on left to Gillswood House take next **L** at exit of wood 'Four Marks 2¹/₄, Medstead 4'.

10 Pass beneath power lines and take next **R** uphill by telegraph pole (NS). At T-j at end of Hawthorn Lane turn **L** then after ¹/₄ mile first **R** at X-roads onto Brightstone Lane.

11 After 1¹/₂ miles at X-roads with A32 in Farringdon **SA** 'Upper Farringdon ¹/₂, Selborne 3'. After almost ¹/₂ mile first **L** on Church Road 'West Worldham 2¹/₂, East Worldham 3¹/₂'.

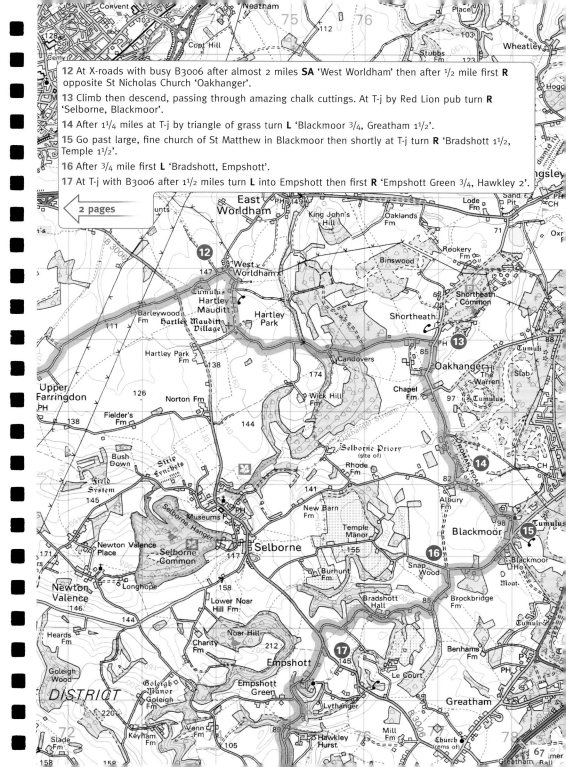

12 At X-roads with busy B3006 after almost 2 miles **SA** 'West Worldham' then after ¹/₂ mile first **R** opposite St Nicholas Church 'Oakhanger'.

13 Climb then descend, passing through amazing chalk cuttings. At T-j by Red Lion pub turn **R** 'Selborne, Blackmoor'.

14 After 1¹/₄ miles at T-j by triangle of grass turn **L** 'Blackmoor ³/₄, Greatham 1¹/₂'.

15 Go past large, fine church of St Matthew in Blackmoor then shortly at T-j turn **R** 'Bradshott 1¹/₂, Temple 1¹/₂'.

16 After ³/₄ mile first **L** 'Bradshott, Empshott'.

17 At T-j with B3006 after 1¹/₂ miles turn **L** into Empshott then first **R** 'Empshott Green ³/₄, Hawkley 2'.

2 pages

From Selborne to the Meon Valley & Cheriton

The village of Selborne is forever associated with two famous men: Gilbert White, the pioneer naturalist who lived here in the 18th century, and Captain Oates, the Antarctic explorer who made such a noble self-sacrifice on Scott's expedition to the South Pole. You can learn about both men at Gilbert White's House & the Oates Museum. Go to www.gilbertwhiteshouse.org.uk for more details. There is also a very good tearoom here. This is one of six rides that explore the dense network of quiet lanes that criss-cross the rolling countryside between the A31 in the west and the A3 in the east. Similar lane rides further east along the base of the South Downs towards Midhurst and Petworth are described in the companion volume *Cycle Tours: Surrey & West Sussex*. The ride runs south then east from Selborne, soon climbing to the highpoint of 755ft (230m). With the exception of one short climb it is downhill all the way to the Meon Valley and a chance for refreshments in the pubs in the pretty village of East Meon. More ups and downs follow as you climb up to Teglease Down for some of the best views of the day before dropping back down into the Meon Valley at Exton.

North to Cheriton and east through Ropley back towards Selborne, the ride threads its way through Hampshire's rich arable landscape past copses of beech trees.

Overview

On-road ● 37 miles / 60 kilometres ● Moderate / Strenuous

Start
Selborne Arms pub, Selborne, southeast of Alton

Parking
Village car park near the Selborne Arms

Busy roads
● 300yds on A272 north of East Meon ❼

● 1 mile on B3046 through Cheriton ❽

Off-road sections
None

Terrain
Undulating, with several climbs of 100-200ft (30-60m) and four longer ones

Nearest railway
Alton, Liss or Petersfield

Refreshments
Selborne
Teashop in Gilbert White's House & the Oates Museum
T: 01420 511275
Queens PH
T: 01420 511454
Selborne Arms PH
T: 01420 511247

South of Colemore
White Horse PH
(Pub with No Name)
T: 01420 588387

East Meon
Ye Olde George PH
T: 01730 823481
Izaak Walton PH
T: 01730 823252

Exton
Shoe Inn
T: 01489 877526

Cheriton
Flowerpots PH
T: 01962 771318

Other rides nearby
Ride 10
Page 62

Ride 11

Ride 12
Page 74

Ride 14
Page 86

Map pages

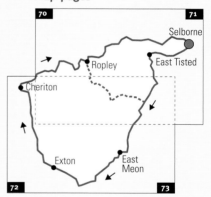

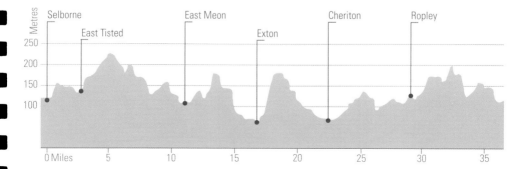

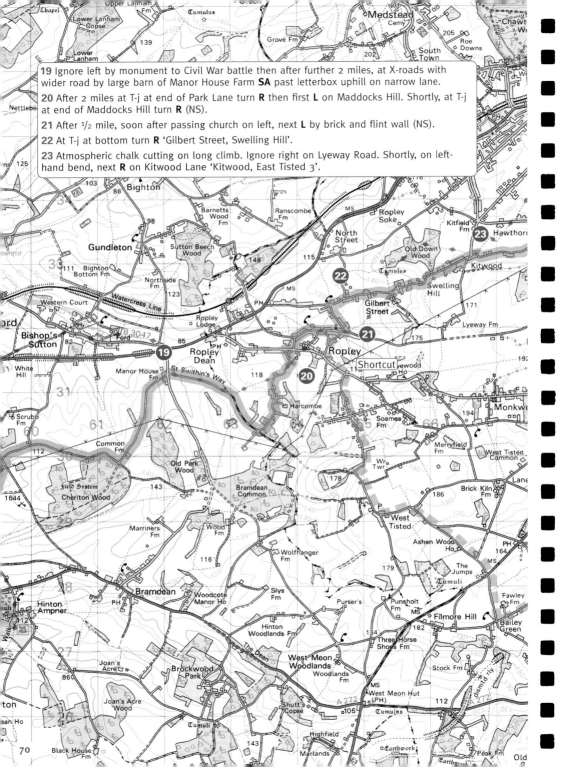

19 Ignore left by monument to Civil War battle then after further 2 miles, at X-roads with wider road by large barn of Manor House Farm **SA** past letterbox uphill on narrow lane.

20 After 2 miles at T-j at end of Park Lane turn **R** then first **L** on Maddocks Hill. Shortly, at T-j at end of Maddocks Hill turn **R** (NS).

21 After ½ mile, soon after passing church on left, next **L** by brick and flint wall (NS).

22 At T-j at bottom turn **R** 'Gilbert Street, Swelling Hill'.

23 Atmospheric chalk cutting on long climb. Ignore right on Lyeway Road. Shortly, on left-hand bend, next **R** on Kitwood Lane 'Kitwood, East Tisted 3'.

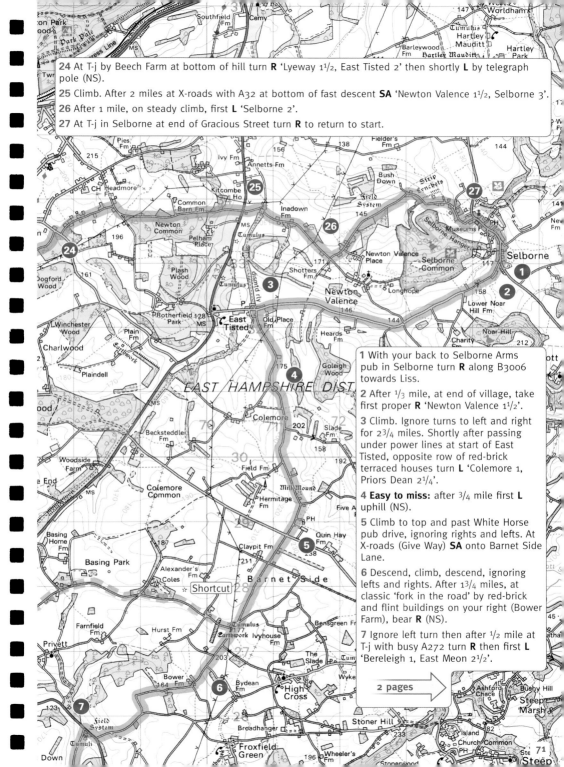

24 At T-j by Beech Farm at bottom of hill turn **R** 'Lyeway 1½, East Tisted 2' then shortly **L** by telegraph pole (NS).

25 Climb. After 2 miles at X-roads with A32 at bottom of fast descent **SA** 'Newton Valence 1½, Selborne 3'.

26 After 1 mile, on steady climb, first **L** 'Selborne 2'.

27 At T-j in Selborne at end of Gracious Street turn **R** to return to start.

1 With your back to Selborne Arms pub in Selborne turn **R** along B3006 towards Liss.

2 After ⅓ mile, at end of village, take first proper **R** 'Newton Valence 1½'.

3 Climb. Ignore turns to left and right for 2¾ miles. Shortly after passing under power lines at start of East Tisted, opposite row of red-brick terraced houses turn **L** 'Colemore 1, Priors Dean 2¼'.

4 Easy to miss: after ¾ mile first **L** uphill (NS).

5 Climb to top and past White Horse pub drive, ignoring rights and lefts. At X-roads (Give Way) **SA** onto Barnet Side Lane.

6 Descend, climb, descend, ignoring lefts and rights. After 1¾ miles, at classic 'fork in the road' by red-brick and flint buildings on your right (Bower Farm), bear **R** (NS).

7 Ignore left turn then after ½ mile at T-j with busy A272 turn **R** then first **L** 'Bereleigh 1, East Meon 2½'.

2 pages ➡

71

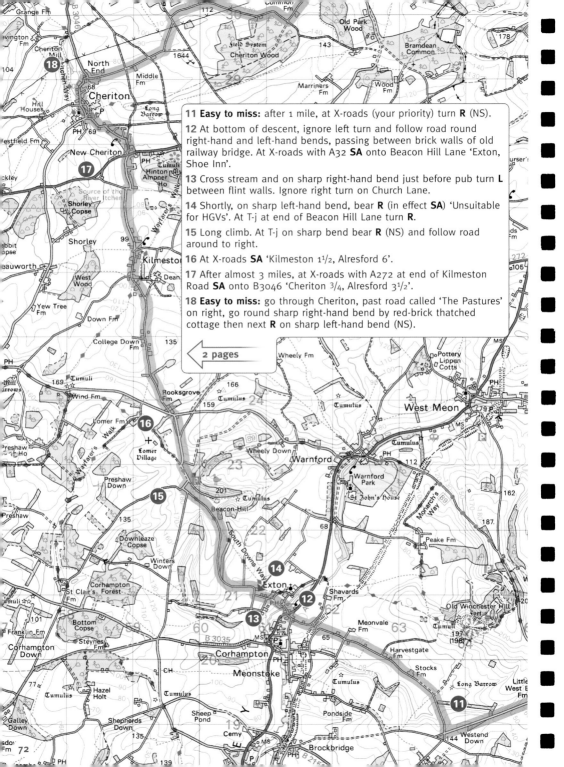

11 Easy to miss: after 1 mile, at X-roads (your priority) turn **R** (NS).

12 At bottom of descent, ignore left turn and follow road round right-hand and left-hand bends, passing between brick walls of old railway bridge. At X-roads with A32 **SA** onto Beacon Hill Lane 'Exton, Shoe Inn'.

13 Cross stream and on sharp right-hand bend just before pub turn **L** between flint walls. Ignore right turn on Church Lane.

14 Shortly, on sharp left-hand bend, bear **R** (in effect **SA**) 'Unsuitable for HGVs'. At T-j at end of Beacon Hill Lane turn **R**.

15 Long climb. At T-j on sharp bend bear **R** (NS) and follow road around to right.

16 At X-roads **SA** 'Kilmeston 1½, Alresford 6'.

17 After almost 3 miles, at X-roads with A272 at end of Kilmeston Road **SA** onto B3046 'Cheriton ¾, Alresford 3½'.

18 Easy to miss: go through Cheriton, past road called 'The Pastures' on right, go round sharp right-hand bend by red-brick thatched cottage then next **R** on sharp left-hand bend (NS).

← 2 pages

72

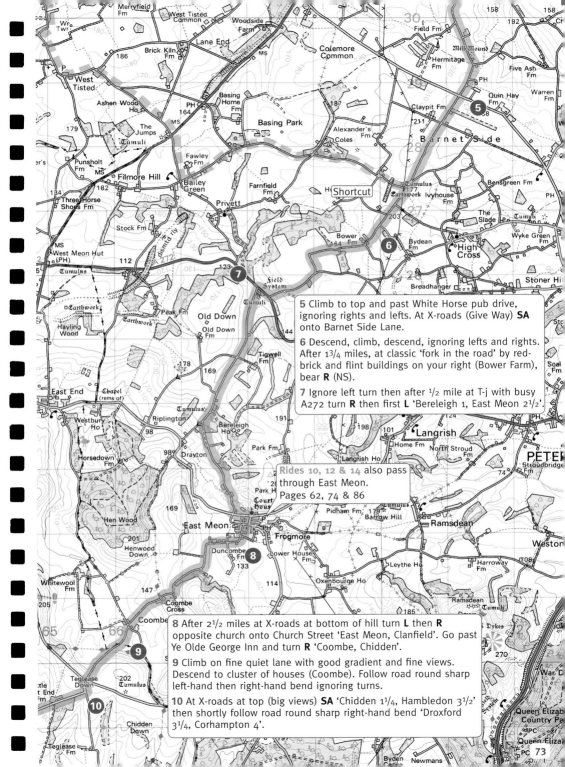

Shortcut

5 Climb to top and past White Horse pub drive, ignoring rights and lefts. At X-roads (Give Way) **SA** onto Barnet Side Lane.

6 Descend, climb, descend, ignoring lefts and rights. After 1¾ miles, at classic 'fork in the road' by red-brick and flint buildings on your right (Bower Farm), bear **R** (NS).

7 Ignore left turn then after ½ mile at T-j with busy A272 turn **R** then first **L** 'Bereleigh 1, East Meon 2½'.

Rides **10, 12 & 14** also pass through East Meon.
Pages 62, 74 & 86

8 After 2½ miles at X-roads at bottom of hill turn **L** then **R** opposite church onto Church Street 'East Meon, Clanfield'. Go past Ye Olde George Inn and turn **R** 'Coombe, Chidden'.

9 Climb on fine quiet lane with good gradient and fine views. Descend to cluster of houses (Coombe). Follow road round sharp left-hand then right-hand bend ignoring turns.

10 At X-roads at top (big views) **SA** 'Chidden 1¼, Hambledon 3½' then shortly follow road round sharp right-hand bend 'Droxford 3¼, Corhampton 4'.

Petersfield
& the Meon Valley

There are several rides in the area lying between the A3 in the east and the A31 in the west – this is not surprising bearing in mind its dense network of beautiful wooded lanes through the rolling Hampshire countryside. The four main roads in the area (the A3, A31, A272 and A32) must carry 90% of the traffic, leaving most of the lanes a delight to ride on. Petersfield is a market town with handsome Georgian houses in Sheep Street and The Spain, the names of which recall

the medieval woollen trade between England and Spain. In the early 19th century the town was a staging post between London and Portsmouth. The exit from Petersfield is the busiest road on the whole route so do not be disheartened – it is not representative of the rest of the ride. Before long you join much quieter lanes along the base of the South Downs. Glide down the Meon Valley before turning north and facing a series of climbs and descents through West Tisted and Ropley to

Farringdon. Selborne is one of the highlights of the ride and it is worth stopping at Gilbert White's House & the Oates Museum, home of the famous naturalist, for its excellent tearoom if nothing else. The climb south from Selborne comes in two parts, taking you to the highpoint of the ride near Warren Corner and setting you up for one of the best and longest descents in the book back down into Petersfield.

Overview

On-road ● 35 miles / 56 kilometres ● Moderate / Strenuous

Start
Tourist Information Centre /
Library, Petersfield

Parking
Several Pay & Display car
parks in Petersfield

Busy roads
B2146 out of Petersfield
1 to **2**

Off-road sections
None

Terrain
Undulating with several short
climbs of 100-200ft (30-60m)
and five longer ones

Nearest railway
Petersfield

Refreshments
Petersfield
Lots of choice

Buriton
Master Robert PH
T: 01730 267275
Five Bells PH
T: 01730 263584

East Meon
Ye Olde George PH
T: 01730 823481
Izaak Walton PH
T: 01730 823252

West Meon
Red Lion PH
T: 01730 829264
Thomas Lord PH
T: 01730 829244

Upper Farringdon
Rose & Crown PH
T: 01420 588231

Selborne
Teashop in Gilbert
White's House &
the Oates Museum
T: 01420 511275
Queens PH
T: 01420 511454
Selborne Arms PH
T: 01420 511247

Return to Petersfield
Trooper PH
T: 01730 827293
Cricketers PH
T: 01730 261035

Other rides nearby

Map pages

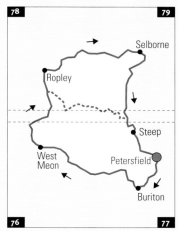

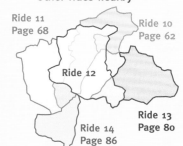

Ride 11
Page 68

Ride 10
Page 62

Ride 12

Ride 13
Page 80

Ride 14
Page 86

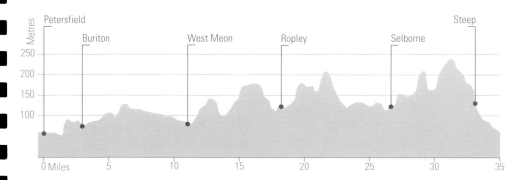

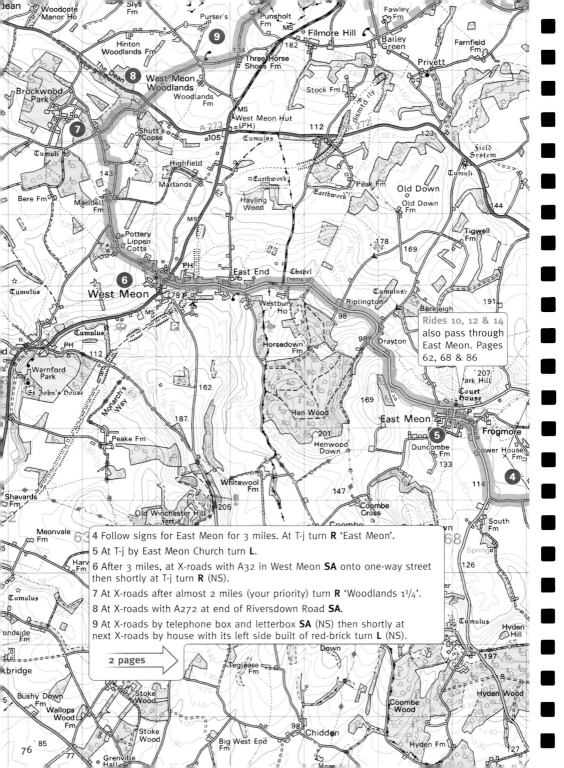

Rides 10, 12 & 14 also pass through East Meon. Pages 62, 68 & 86

4 Follow signs for East Meon for 3 miles. At T-j turn **R** 'East Meon'.

5 At T-j by East Meon Church turn **L**.

6 After 3 miles, at X-roads with A32 in West Meon **SA** onto one-way street then shortly at T-j turn **R** (NS).

7 At X-roads after almost 2 miles (your priority) turn **R** 'Woodlands 1¼'.

8 At X-roads with A272 at end of Riversdown Road **SA**.

9 At X-roads by telephone box and letterbox **SA** (NS) then shortly at next X-roads by house with its left side built of red-brick turn **L** (NS).

2 pages →

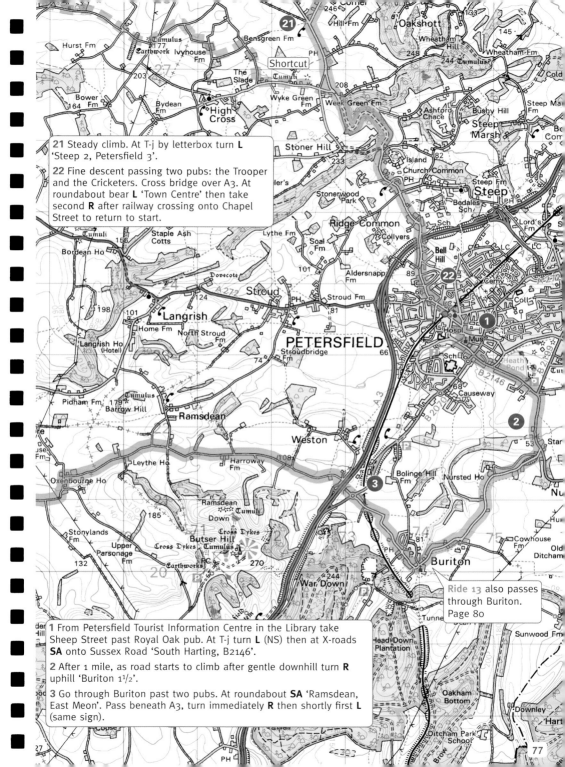

21 Steady climb. At T-j by letterbox turn **L** 'Steep 2, Petersfield 3'.

22 Fine descent passing two pubs: the Trooper and the Cricketers. Cross bridge over A3. At roundabout bear **L** 'Town Centre' then take second **R** after railway crossing onto Chapel Street to return to start.

Ride **13** also passes through Buriton. Page 80

1 From Petersfield Tourist Information Centre in the Library take Sheep Street past Royal Oak pub. At T-j turn **L** (NS) then at X-roads **SA** onto Sussex Road 'South Harting, B2146'.

2 After 1 mile, as road starts to climb after gentle downhill turn **R** uphill 'Buriton 1½'.

3 Go through Buriton past two pubs. At roundabout **SA** 'Ramsdean, East Meon'. Pass beneath A3, turn immediately **R** then shortly first **L** (same sign).

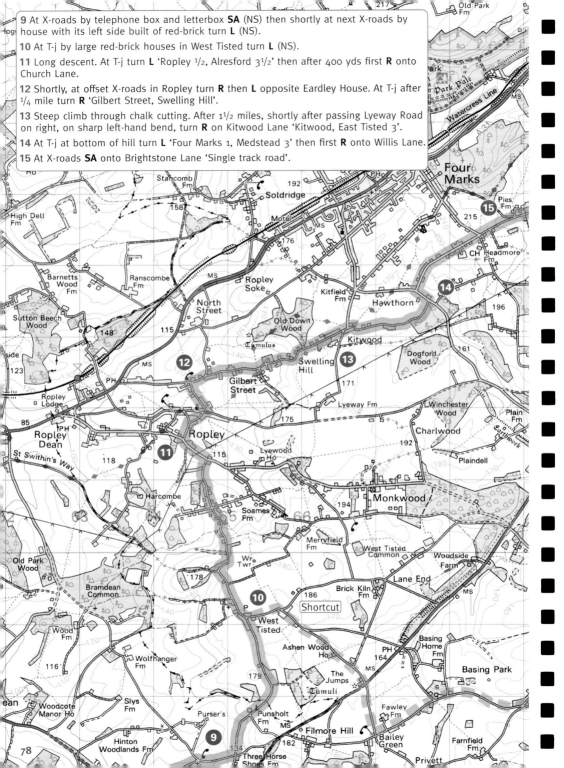

9 At X-roads by telephone box and letterbox **SA** (NS) then shortly at next X-roads by house with its left side built of red-brick turn **L** (NS).

10 At T-j by large red-brick houses in West Tisted turn **L** (NS).

11 Long descent. At T-j turn **L** 'Ropley ½, Alresford 3½' then after 400 yds first **R** onto Church Lane.

12 Shortly, at offset X-roads in Ropley turn **R** then **L** opposite Eardley House. At T-j after ¼ mile turn **R** 'Gilbert Street, Swelling Hill'.

13 Steep climb through chalk cutting. After 1½ miles, shortly after passing Lyeway Road on right, on sharp left-hand bend, turn **R** on Kitwood Lane 'Kitwood, East Tisted 3'.

14 At T-j at bottom of hill turn **L** 'Four Marks 1, Medstead 3' then first **R** onto Willis Lane.

15 At X-roads **SA** onto Brightstone Lane 'Single track road'.

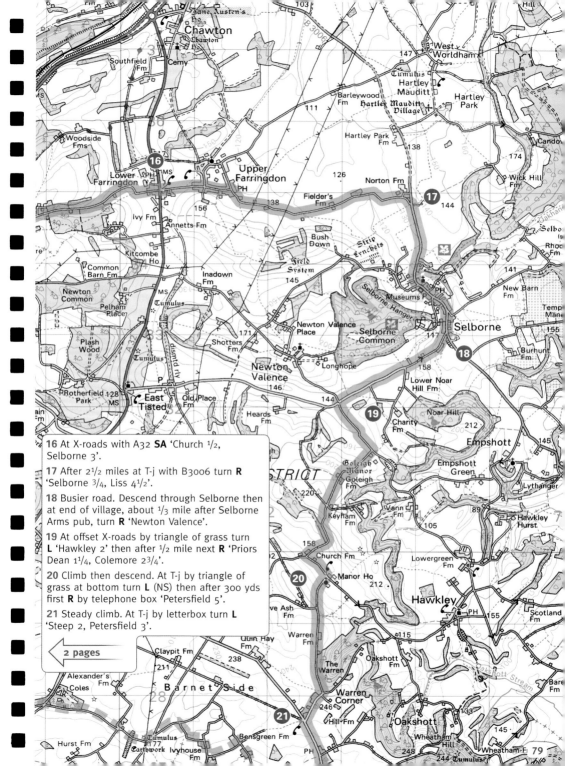

16 At X-roads with A32 **SA** 'Church ½, Selborne 3'.

17 After 2½ miles at T-j with B3006 turn **R** 'Selborne ¾, Liss 4½'.

18 Busier road. Descend through Selborne then at end of village, about ⅓ mile after Selborne Arms pub, turn **R** 'Newton Valence'.

19 At offset X-roads by triangle of grass turn **L** 'Hawkley 2' then after ½ mile next **R** 'Priors Dean 1¼, Colemore 2¾'.

20 Climb then descend. At T-j by triangle of grass at bottom turn **L** (NS) then after 300 yds first **R** by telephone box 'Petersfield 5'.

21 Steady climb. At T-j by letterbox turn **L** 'Steep 2, Petersfield 3'.

2 pages

Wooded lanes through the Rother Valley from Buriton

Much as Rides 3 & 4 describe imaginary wheels around the hubs of Andover and Basingstoke, so too does this ride form a circuit around Petersfield, avoiding the traffic inevitably associated with a town of its size. Time is almost evenly split between Hampshire and West Sussex on this ride but the linking theme is the River Rother, either crossing its tributaries that cut through the thickly wooded slopes to the west of Petersfield, or running along the wider valley floor formed by the river between Petersfield and Midhurst. The River Rother flows into the River Arun, one of few that cut through the great chalk whaleback of the South Downs, emerging at the sea at Littlehampton. Be aware that route-finding along the steep and winding lanes around Steep, Oakshott and Hawkley can be particularly challenging so pay good attention to the map and instructions. There are splendid views of the steep hillsides cloaked in majestic broadleaf woodlands. You leave Hampshire for West Sussex in Rake and the River Rother is crossed just south of Chithurst. Ahead of you are the South Downs, rising to 800ft (242m) on Beacon Hill above East Harting. A meandering lane route through West Harting and Goose Green minimises time spent on the busy B2146 on your return to Buriton. Rides further east from here are described in the companion volume *Cycle Tours: Surrey & West Sussex.*

Overview
On-road ● 28 miles / 45 kilometres ● Easy / Moderate

Start
Buriton, 3 miles south
of Petersfield

Parking
By the church in Buriton

Busy roads
● 450yds on A272 at
Stroud **5**

● 600yds on B3006 north
of Liss **10**

● 300yds on A272 south
of Chithurst **19**

Off-road sections
None

Terrain Undulating with a
few short climbs of 100-200ft
(30-60m) but no longer ones

Nearest railway
Liss

Refreshments
Buriton
Master Robert PH
T: 01730 267275
Five Bells PH
T: 01730 263584

Stroud
Seven Stars PH
T: 01730 264122

Steep
Cricketers PH
T: 01730 261035

Hawkley
Hawkley Inn
T: 01730 827205

Liss Forest
Temple Inn
T: 01730 892134

Rake
Sun Inn
T: 01730 892115
Flying Bull PH
T: 01730 892285

Trotton
Keepers Arms PH
T: 01730 813724

Other rides nearby

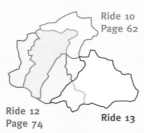

Ride 10
Page 62

Ride 12
Page 74

Ride 13

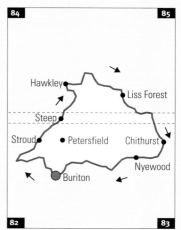

Map pages

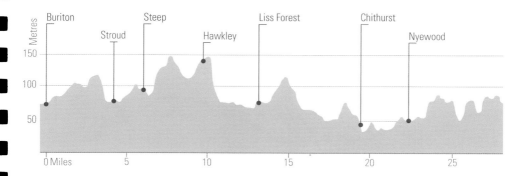

Ride 12 also passes through Buriton. Page 74

24 After further 3/4 mile at T-j with pylons in field to right, turn **L** (NS).

25 At T-j with B2146 by 'Hampshire' sign turn **R**.

26 Climb then descend on busy road. After almost 3/4 mile first **L** 'Buriton 1 1/2' to return to the start.

1 From Buriton church head northwest towards A3 past pubs in village.

2 At roundabout **SA** 'Ramsdean, East Meon'. Pass beneath A3, turn immediately **R** then shortly first **L** (same sign).

3 Easy to miss: after 1 3/4 miles take first proper **R** (no sign but the turn is opposite 'Buriton / East Meon' sign tucked in hedgerow).

4 After 1/2 mile, turn **R** by triangle of grass 'Petersfield 3'.

5 Follow for 1 1/2 miles. At T-j with A272 at end of Ramsdean Road by Seven Stars pub turn **R** 'Petersfield 2' then after 1/4 mile first **L** onto Ridge Common Lane 'Steep 1 1/2'. Use pavement if road is busy but cross before turn where you can see traffic clearly in both directions.

2 pages ⟹

82

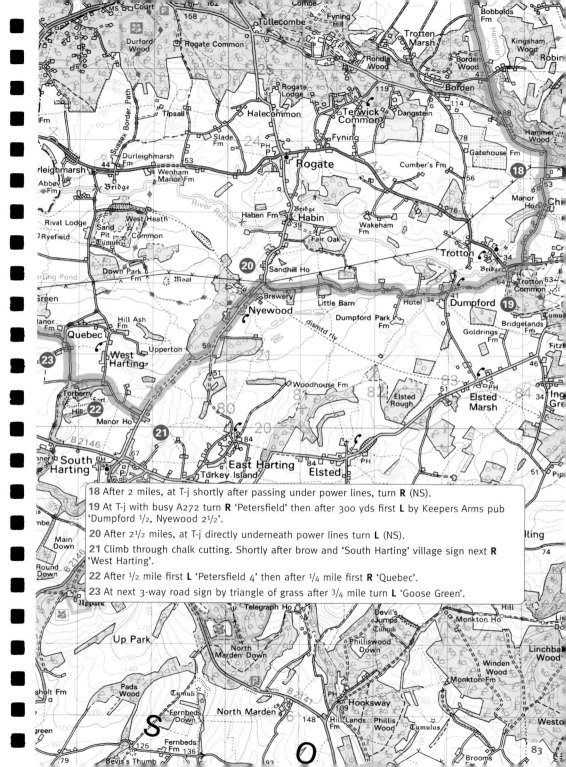

18 After 2 miles, at T-j shortly after passing under power lines, turn **R** (NS).

19 At T-j with busy A272 turn **R** 'Petersfield' then after 300 yds first **L** by Keepers Arms pub 'Dumpford ½, Nyewood 2½'.

20 After 2½ miles, at T-j directly underneath power lines turn **L** (NS).

21 Climb through chalk cutting. Shortly after brow and 'South Harting' village sign next **R** 'West Harting'.

22 After ½ mile first **L** 'Petersfield 4' then after ¼ mile first **R** 'Quebec'.

23 At next 3-way road sign by triangle of grass after ¾ mile turn **L** 'Goose Green'.

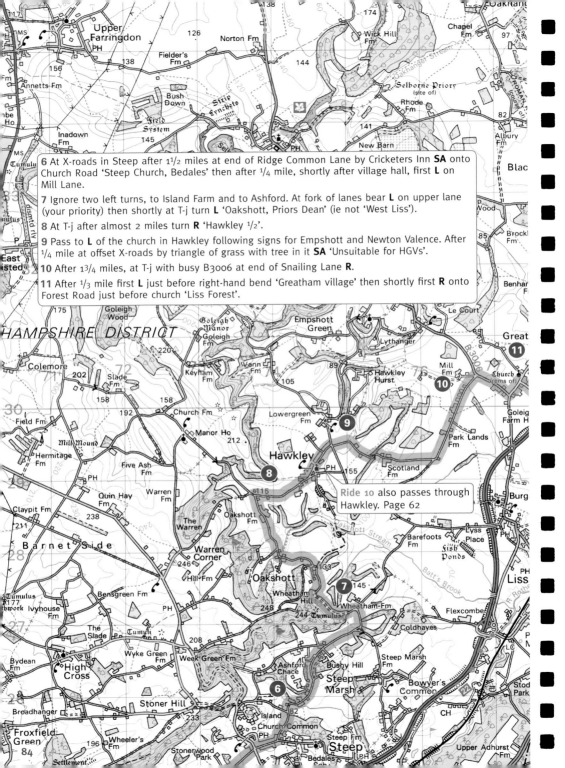

6 At X-roads in Steep after 1½ miles at end of Ridge Common Lane by Cricketers Inn **SA** onto Church Road 'Steep Church, Bedales' then after ¼ mile, shortly after village hall, first **L** on Mill Lane.

7 Ignore two left turns, to Island Farm and to Ashford. At fork of lanes bear **L** on upper lane (your priority) then shortly at T-j turn **L** 'Oakshott, Priors Dean' (ie not 'West Liss').

8 At T-j after almost 2 miles turn **R** 'Hawkley ½'.

9 Pass to **L** of the church in Hawkley following signs for Empshott and Newton Valence. After ¼ mile at offset X-roads by triangle of grass with tree in it **SA** 'Unsuitable for HGVs'.

10 After 1¾ miles, at T-j with busy B3006 at end of Snailing Lane **R**.

11 After ⅓ mile first **L** just before right-hand bend 'Greatham village' then shortly first **R** onto Forest Road just before church 'Liss Forest'.

Ride 10 also passes through Hawkley. Page 62

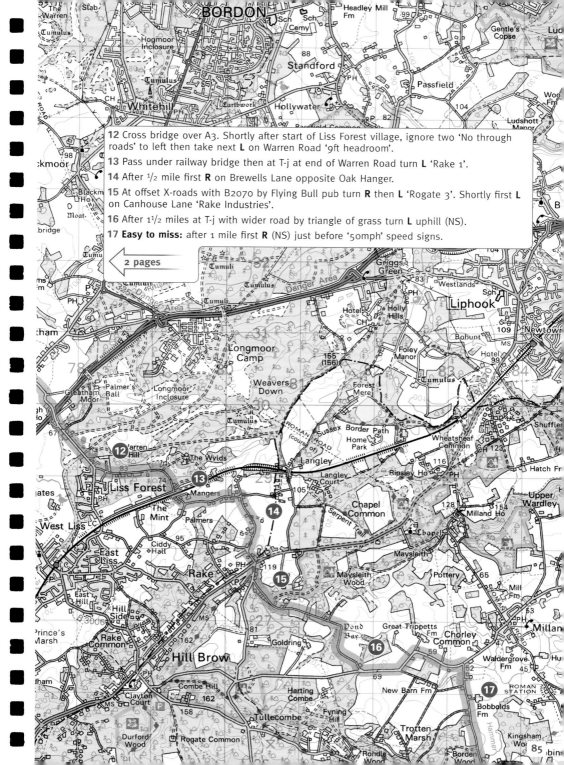

12 Cross bridge over A3. Shortly after start of Liss Forest village, ignore two 'No through roads' to left then take next **L** on Warren Road '9ft headroom'.

13 Pass under railway bridge then at T-j at end of Warren Road turn **L** 'Rake 1'.

14 After ¹/₂ mile first **R** on Brewells Lane opposite Oak Hanger.

15 At offset X-roads with B2070 by Flying Bull pub turn **R** then **L** 'Rogate 3'. Shortly first **L** on Canhouse Lane 'Rake Industries'.

16 After 1¹/₂ miles at T-j with wider road by triangle of grass turn **L** uphill (NS).

17 **Easy to miss:** after 1 mile first **R** (NS) just before '50mph' speed signs.

2 pages

East Meon south to Hambledon

As mentioned earlier, East Meon is one of the finest cycling bases in Hampshire, surrounded as it is by a delightful network of rolling wooded country lanes that carry very little traffic. It is an attractive village on the River Meon, once fished by Izaak Walton, author of *The Compleat Angler*. The Norman Church of All Saints has a magnificent font in black Tournai marble with carvings depicting Creation, Temptation and the Expulsion from Eden. Climb gently out of East Meon up a wide valley with a steep grassy escarpment up to the right. Arable fields turn to pasture and the gradient steepens. About 5 miles south of East Meon you pass a memorial stone to the Hambledon Cricket Club, founded in 1760 and the birthplace of cricket. It was here that the rules of modern cricket were evolved. Thomas Lord, founder of Lord's Cricket Ground in London, is buried in nearby West Meon. Hambledon village itself offers the chance of a tea or coffee break in the village stores. On the outskirts of the village on a south-facing slope lies one of England's most successful vineyards. A steady climb from here takes you up onto Teglease Down with great views from the summit and along the ridge. Drop down into the Meon Valley at West Meon and follow the valley eastwards back to the start.

Overview

On-road ● 23 miles / 37 kilometres ● Moderate

Start
East Meon, off the A272 to the west of Petersfield

Parking
Follow signs for free car park from Ye Olde George Inn on the road towards Coombe and Chidden

Busy roads
450yds on A32 through West Meon **14**

Off-road sections
None

Terrain
Undulating with several short climbs of 100-200ft (30-60m) and two longer ones

Nearest railway
Petersfield

Refreshments
East Meon
Ye Olde George PH
T: 01730 823481
Izaak Walton PH
T: 01730 823252

Hambledon Cricket Ground
Bat & Ball PH
T: 02392 632692

Hambledon
Tea room in the village stores

Soberton
White Lion PH
T: 01489 877346

Droxford
Hurdles PH
T: 01489 877451

West Meon
Red Lion PH
T: 01730 829264
Thomas Lord PH
T: 01730 829244

Other rides nearby

Ride 10
Page 62

Ride 11
Page 68

Ride 12
Page 74

Ride 14

Map pages

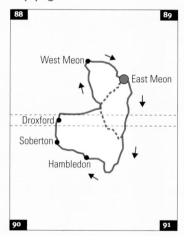

88   89

West Meon

East Meon

Droxford

Soberton

Hambledon

90   91

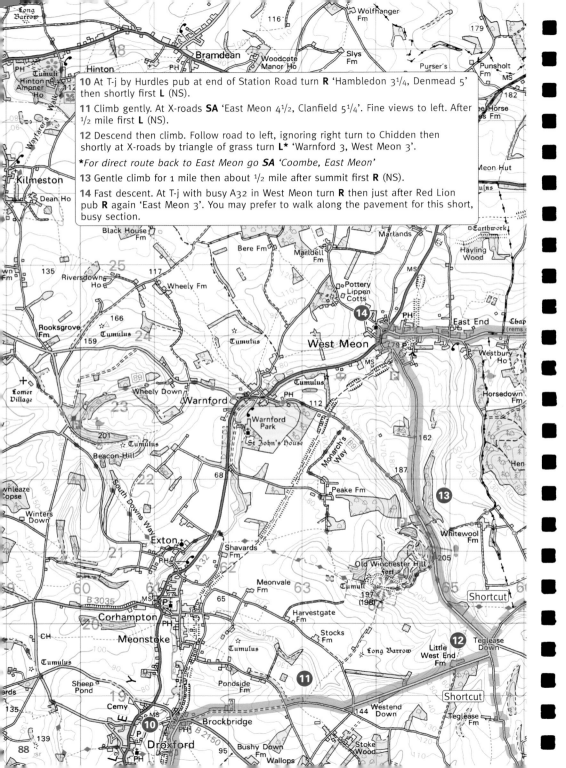

10 At T-j by Hurdles pub at end of Station Road turn **R** 'Hambledon 3¼, Denmead 5' then shortly first **L** (NS).

11 Climb gently. At X-roads **SA** 'East Meon 4½, Clanfield 5¼'. Fine views to left. After ½ mile first **L** (NS).

12 Descend then climb. Follow road to left, ignoring right turn to Chidden then shortly at X-roads by triangle of grass turn **L*** 'Warnford 3, West Meon 3'.

For direct route back to East Meon go SA 'Coombe, East Meon'

13 Gentle climb for 1 mile then about ½ mile after summit first **R** (NS).

14 Fast descent. At T-j with busy A32 in West Meon turn **R** then just after Red Lion pub **R** again 'East Meon 3'. You may prefer to walk along the pavement for this short, busy section.

15 Follow road for 3½ miles back to start in East Meon, turning **R** at church to return to Olde George Inn.

Rides **10, 11 & 12** also pass through East Meon. Pages 62, 68 & 74

Shortcut

1 From Ye Olde George Inn in East Meon follow road round towards Clanfield and Horndean.

2 Climb gently then more steadily. After 2 miles, on left-hand bend turn **R** to continue steeply uphill then at X-roads **SA** onto Hyden Farm Lane 'Hambledon 3¾, Denmead 5'.

2 pages →

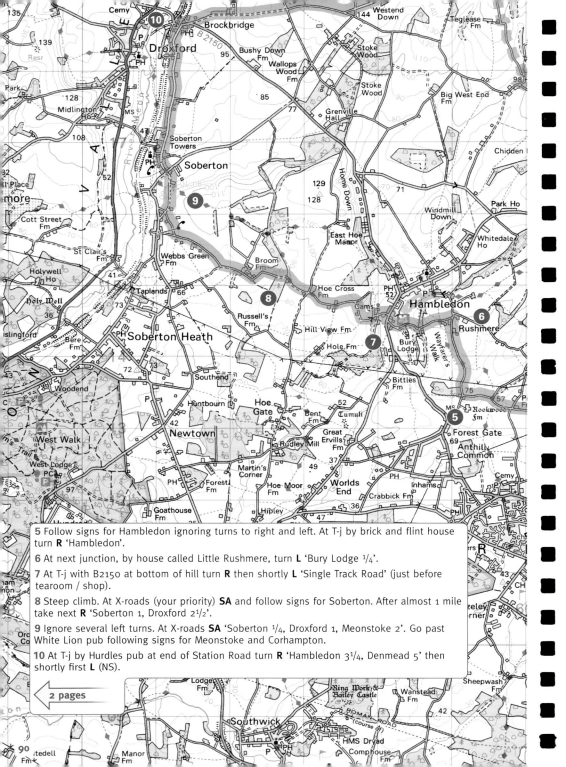

5 Follow signs for Hambledon ignoring turns to right and left. At T-j by brick and flint house turn **R** 'Hambledon'.

6 At next junction, by house called Little Rushmere, turn **L** 'Bury Lodge ¼'.

7 At T-j with B2150 at bottom of hill turn **R** then shortly **L** 'Single Track Road' (just before tearoom / shop).

8 Steep climb. At X-roads (your priority) **SA** and follow signs for Soberton. After almost 1 mile take next **R** 'Soberton 1, Droxford 2½'.

9 Ignore several left turns. At X-roads **SA** 'Soberton ¼, Droxford 1, Meonstoke 2'. Go past White Lion pub following signs for Meonstoke and Corhampton.

10 At T-j by Hurdles pub at end of Station Road turn **R** 'Hambledon 3¼, Denmead 5' then shortly first **L** (NS).

⬅ 2 pages

3 Fine woodland descent. At X-roads by Bat & Ball pub **SA** onto Old Mill Lane 'Denmead 3½'.

4 Long, gentle descent down 'hidden' shallow valley. Short climb, second descent. **Easy to miss:** immediately after passing under second set of power lines turn **R** (just before triangle of grass with 4-way signpost by Kimberley House).

Around the Isle of Wight on railway paths & quiet roads

The Isle of Wight has made real efforts to promote cycling with the conversion of several old railways to recreational use, the longest of which runs from Sandown to Newport (partly used in this ride), with others connecting Newport to Cowes (also used), Shanklin to Wroxall and Yarmouth to Freshwater. There is also a superb mountain bike ride along the Tennyson Trail in the west of the island (see off-road Ride 5, page 114). Finding quiet rides on the

lane network is more of a challenge as almost all the roads on the island carry reasonable levels of traffic, especially during school holidays. Head north from Cowes for some fine views out over the Solent before turning southwest through Porchfield on one of the (unavoidable) busier stretches of road. Crossing the spine of the island on the road through Brighstone Forest offers some of the best views of the day out over the English Channel, and

an excellent coffee stop in Brighstone village. The flattest and quietest lanes of the day lead southeast through Yafford and Atherfield. The ride turns north to Merstone to join the railway path, with its fine sculptures, taking you right to the edge of Newport. You will need your wits about you to navigate through town to find the start of the final section, the railway path that leads back into Cowes, with wide views over the yachts moored in the River Medina.

Overview

On-road ● 34 miles / 55 kilometres ● Moderate

Start
The junction of Market Hill and High Street in Cowes on the Isle of Wight

Parking
Several Pay & Display car parks in Cowes

Busy roads
The ride uses streets in Cowes and Newport. The 'minor' road between Rew Street and Shalfleet (used for 3½ miles) can get busy **3** to **5**

Off-road sections
● Railway path from Merstone to the southern edge of Newport

● Railway path from northern edge of Newport to Cowes

Terrain
Flat along the two railway paths. Otherwise generally undulating with a few climbs of 100-200ft (30-60m) and one longer, steeper climb of 390ft (118m) up through Brighstone Forest

Nearest ferry
Cowes

Refreshments
Cowes
Lots of choice

Porchfield
Sportsman's Rest PH
T: 01983 522044

Calbourne
Sun PH
T: 01983 531231

Brighstone
Three Bishops PH
T: 01983 740226
Tea Rooms
T: 01983 740370

Newport
Lots of choice

Other rides nearby
At Instruction 15, instead of turning left on the cyclepath turn right on the traffic-free trail to visit Sandown, or add on an extra loop via Alverstone - Brading - Upton - Wootton - East Cowes, using minor roads

Map pages

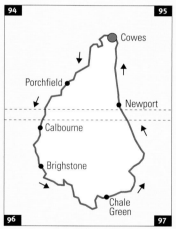

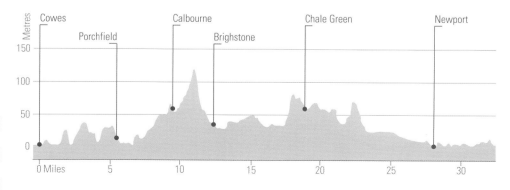

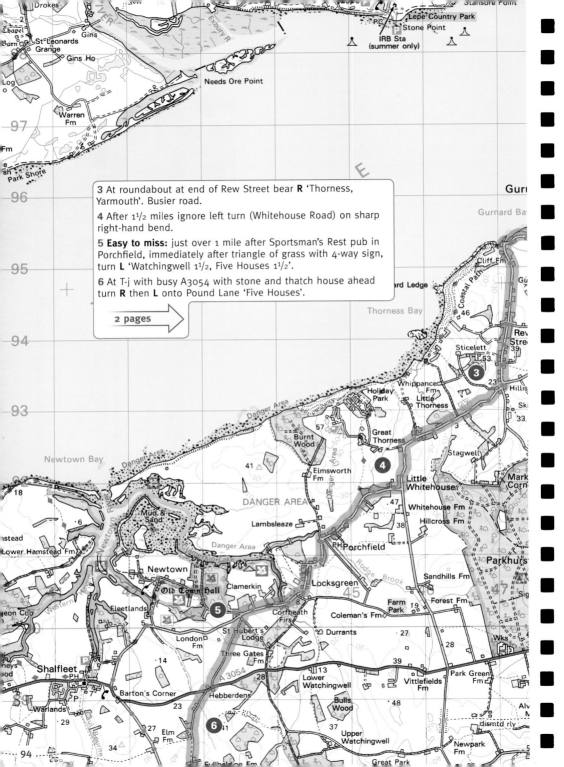

3 At roundabout at end of Rew Street bear **R** 'Thorness, Yarmouth'. Busier road.

4 After 1½ miles ignore left turn (Whitehouse Road) on sharp right-hand bend.

5 Easy to miss: just over 1 mile after Sportsman's Rest pub in Porchfield, immediately after triangle of grass with 4-way sign, turn **L** 'Watchingwell 1½, Five Houses 1½'.

6 At T-j with busy A3054 with stone and thatch house ahead turn **R** then **L** onto Pound Lane 'Five Houses'.

2 pages →

1 From north end of (pedestrianised) High Street in centre of Cowes at junction with (bottom of) Market Hill, head north away from town centre. After 1/4 mile turn **R** on Queens Road.

2 Lovely coastline section. Climb steeply away from sea. Shortly after Shore Road changes name to Worsley Road turn **R** on Solent View Road.

22 At T-j at end of trail turn **R** then at mini-roundabout **L** 'Cowes Cycle Route'. At next mini-roundabout at junction of Bernard Road and Bridge Road bear **L** 'Cowes Cycle Route'.

23 At T-j at end of Arctic Road turn **R** then at next T-j (with Mill Road) turn **R** downhill then second **L** onto West Hill Road.

24 At T-j at end of West Hill Road turn **R** then shortly turn **L** and dismount to walk along pedestrianised Shooters Hill for 600 yds through centre of Cowes back to start.

19 Follow Quay Street round to left as it becomes Sea Street then shortly after red-brick building on your right next **R** 'Cowes Cycle Route' onto Little London, opposite Sea Street car park.

20 Go past Bargeman's Rest pub on contraflow cycle lane and follow road up to **L** at end of Odessa Boatyard. At T-j by Plumb Center turn **R**.

21 At roundabout **SA** onto Manners View then shortly bear **R** to join traffic-free trail to Cowes. Follow trail for 3 miles.

17 Lots of instructions through Newport: follow road round to right. At T-j at end of Medina Avenue **L** onto St Georges Approach. Get into the right-hand lane to turn **R** into Church Litten.

18 At traffic lights in centre of town turn **L** by Prince of Wales pub. Go past Somerfield and at T-j turn **R** towards square. At end of square turn **R** by lions monument onto High Street then shortly **L** by Guildhall / Tourist Information Centre 'Cowes via cycletrack'.

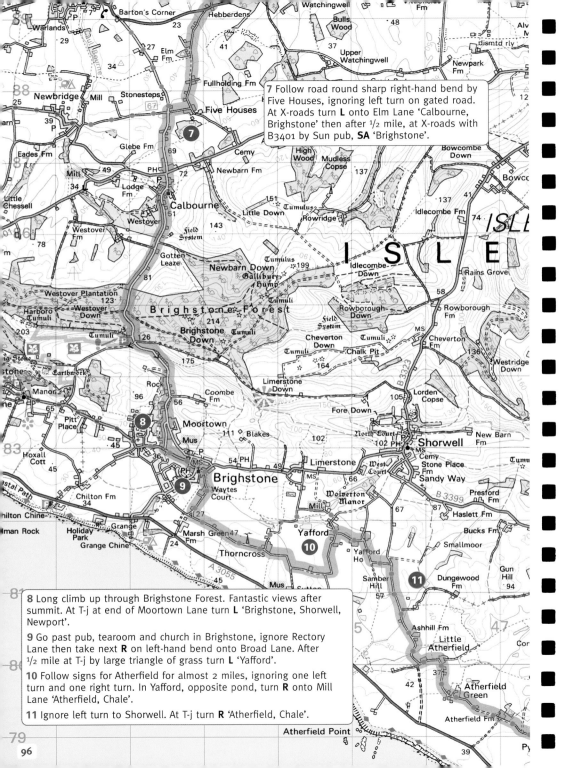

7 Follow road round sharp right-hand bend by Five Houses, ignoring left turn on gated road. At X-roads turn **L** onto Elm Lane 'Calbourne, Brighstone' then after ½ mile, at X-roads with B3401 by Sun pub, **SA** 'Brighstone'.

8 Long climb up through Brighstone Forest. Fantastic views after summit. At T-j at end of Moortown Lane turn **L** 'Brighstone, Shorwell, Newport'.

9 Go past pub, tearoom and church in Brighstone, ignore Rectory Lane then take next **R** on left-hand bend onto Broad Lane. After ½ mile at T-j by large triangle of grass turn **L** 'Yafford'.

10 Follow signs for Atherfield for almost 2 miles, ignoring one left turn and one right turn. In Yafford, opposite pond, turn **R** onto Mill Lane 'Atherfield, Chale'.

11 Ignore left turn to Shorwell. At T-j turn **R** 'Atherfield, Chale'.

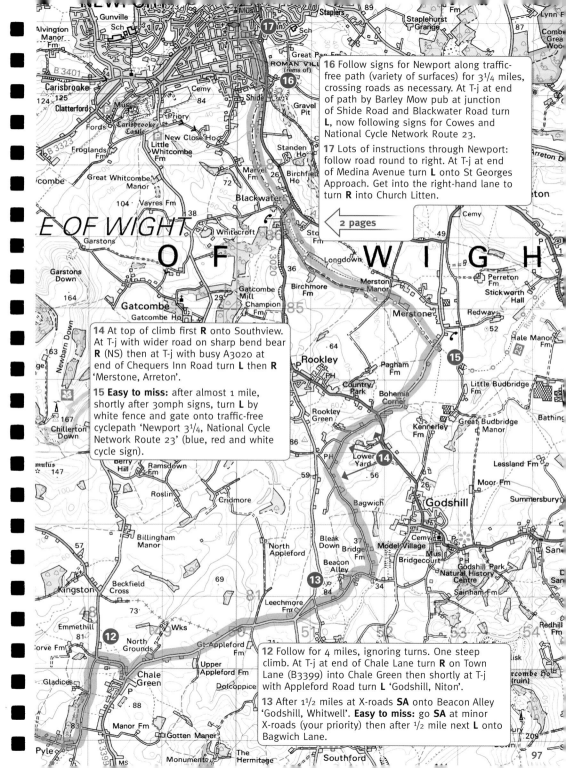

16 Follow signs for Newport along traffic-free path (variety of surfaces) for 3¹/₄ miles, crossing roads as necessary. At T-j at end of path by Barley Mow pub at junction of Shide Road and Blackwater Road turn **L**, now following signs for Cowes and National Cycle Network Route 23.

17 Lots of instructions through Newport: follow road round to right. At T-j at end of Medina Avenue turn **L** onto St Georges Approach. Get into the right-hand lane to turn **R** into Church Litten.

2 pages

14 At top of climb first **R** onto Southview. At T-j with wider road on sharp bend bear **R** (NS) then at T-j with busy A3020 at end of Chequers Inn Road turn **L** then **R** 'Merstone, Arreton'.

15 Easy to miss: after almost 1 mile, shortly after 30mph signs, turn **L** by white fence and gate onto traffic-free cyclepath 'Newport 3¹/₄, National Cycle Network Route 23' (blue, red and white cycle sign).

12 Follow for 4 miles, ignoring turns. One steep climb. At T-j at end of Chale Lane turn **R** on Town Lane (B3399) into Chale Green then shortly at T-j with Appleford Road turn **L** 'Godshill, Niton'.

13 After 1¹/₂ miles at X-roads **SA** onto Beacon Alley 'Godshill, Whitwell'. **Easy to miss:** go **SA** at minor X-roads (your priority) then after ¹/₂ mile next **L** onto Bagwich Lane.

Hurstbourne Tarrant & Inkpen Hill

A long, gentle uphill on a quiet lane gives you plenty of time to warm up for the challenging off-road woodland climb to the mast on Combe Hill, all rideable in good conditions. Views open up to the north over the valley formed by the River Kennet with echoes of the South Downs ridge overlooking the Sussex Weald. Go past the gibbet and imagine the hanged man swinging! You've had a good climb, now enjoy a fine descent from Inkpen Hill

down the dry valley towards Linkenholt. Good, wide stone-based 'conversational' tracks are followed back to Ibthorpe to rejoin the outward route. At 975ft (297m), Walbury Hill is the highest piece of chalk in Southern England, higher than anything on the North and South Downs. There is a lot of excellent riding to the south of Walbury Hill and Inkpen Hill. However, the vast majority of the byway running east-west along the top of the ridge is unuseable because 4x4 vehicles have wrecked

it. This is marked on the Ordnance Survey map with a series of small red crosses all the way from the A34 in the east (south of Highclere), over Walbury Hill and Inkpen Hill to Botley Down in the west (southeast of Great Bedwyn). Easier off-road rides in the area include tracks in Savernake Forest, the Marlborough to Chiseldon Railway Path, and the Kennet and Avon Canal towpath from Newbury to Reading.

Overview

Off-road ● 17 miles / 27 kilometres ● Moderate / Strenuous

Start
Hurstbourne Tarrant, north of Andover on the A343

Parking
Free car park opposite the church on the B3048 on the east side of Hurstbourne Tarrant

Busy roads
None

Terrain
This is the highest part of Hampshire. One long climb of 655ft (199m) from the start to the highpoint ❶ to ❼ with a steep middle section up through woodland to the masts on Combe Hill. One short 165ft (50m) climb ⓫ on the return leg up to Linkenholt

Nearest railway
Whitchurch or Hungerford

Refreshments
Hurstbourne Tarrant
George & Dragon PH
T: 01264 736277

**Upton
(just off the route)**
Crown Inn
T: 01264 736265

Map pages

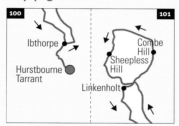

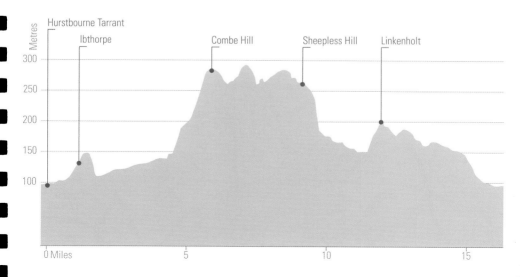

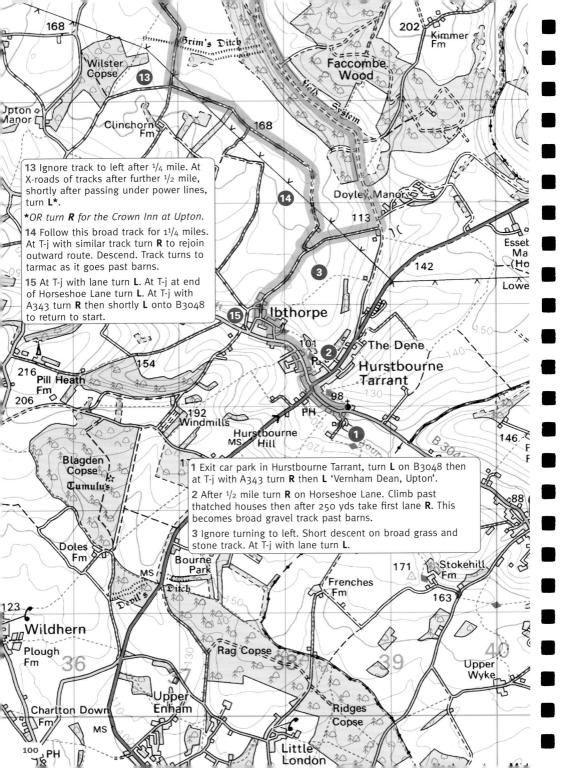

13 Ignore track to left after ¼ mile. At X-roads of tracks after further ½ mile, shortly after passing under power lines, turn **L***.

*OR turn R for the Crown Inn at Upton.

14 Follow this broad track for 1¼ miles. At T-j with similar track turn **R** to rejoin outward route. Descend. Track turns to tarmac as it goes past barns.

15 At T-j with lane turn **L**. At T-j at end of Horseshoe Lane turn **L**. At T-j with A343 turn **R** then shortly **L** onto B3048 to return to start.

1 Exit car park in Hurstbourne Tarrant, turn **L** on B3048 then at T-j with A343 turn **R** then **L** 'Vernham Dean, Upton'.

2 After ½ mile turn **R** on Horseshoe Lane. Climb past thatched houses then after 250 yds take first lane **R**. This becomes broad gravel track past barns.

3 Ignore turning to left. Short descent on broad grass and stone track. At T-j with lane turn **L**.

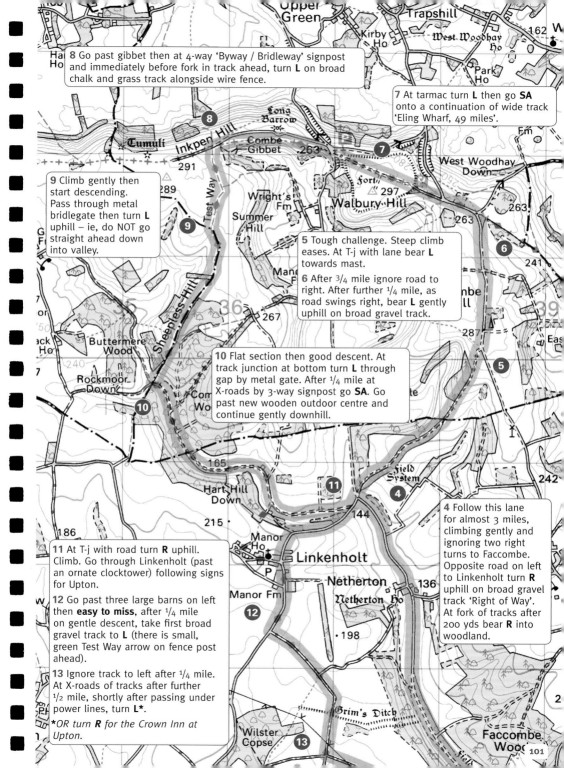

8 Go past gibbet then at 4-way 'Byway / Bridleway' signpost and immediately before fork in track ahead, turn **L** on broad chalk and grass track alongside wire fence.

7 At tarmac turn **L** then go **SA** onto a continuation of wide track 'Eling Wharf, 49 miles'.

9 Climb gently then start descending. Pass through metal bridlegate then turn **L** uphill – ie, do NOT go straight ahead down into valley.

5 Tough challenge. Steep climb eases. At T-j with lane bear **L** towards mast.

6 After ³/₄ mile ignore road to right. After further ¹/₄ mile, as road swings right, bear **L** gently uphill on broad gravel track.

10 Flat section then good descent. At track junction at bottom turn **L** through gap by metal gate. After ¹/₄ mile at X-roads by 3-way signpost go **SA**. Go past new wooden outdoor centre and continue gently downhill.

4 Follow this lane for almost 3 miles, climbing gently and ignoring two right turns to Faccombe. Opposite road on left to Linkenholt turn **R** uphill on broad gravel track 'Right of Way'. At fork of tracks after 200 yds bear **R** into woodland.

11 At T-j with road turn **R** uphill. Climb. Go through Linkenholt (past an ornate clocktower) following signs for Upton.

12 Go past three large barns on left then **easy to miss**, after ¹/₄ mile on gentle descent, take first broad gravel track to **L** (there is small, green Test Way arrow on fence post ahead).

13 Ignore track to left after ¹/₄ mile. At X-roads of tracks after further ¹/₂ mile, shortly after passing under power lines, turn **L***.

*OR turn **R** for the Crown Inn at Upton.

101

Queen Elizabeth Country Park & the South Downs Way

The Forestry Commission holding at Queen Elizabeth Country Park to the south of Petersfield is a focus for mountain biking in the area. There are waymarked trails in the surrounding woodland and a good visitor centre with café attached. This route stays on the east side of the A3, heading south towards Chalton on a narrow chalk track before turning east and following one of those wide stone tracks that you can just imagine a horse and carriage rolling along in a typical period drama. The route stays on broad chalk and stone tracks, soon joining the South Downs Way as it heads west on a rollercoaster ride back to the visitor centre, finishing with a fine long descent. To the west of the visitor centre, accessed via a subway beneath the A3, lies Butser Hill, which offers a good challenging climb straight up its steep grassy slopes to the mast at the top. To the east of the visitor centre there is a huge range of bridleway and byway options criss-crossing the countryside lying to the south of the escarpment all the way to the River Arun and beyond. For easier off-road rides there is the Meon Valley Trail on an old railway line from Wickham to East Meon, the Centurion Way north of Chichester, the Salterns Way south of Chichester or the waymarked trail in Alice Holt Forest, southwest of Farnham.

Overview

Off-road ● 10 miles / 16 kilometres ● Moderate

Start
Queen Elizabeth Country Park, on the A3 southwest of Petersfield

Parking
Pay & Display car parks by the Visitor Centre

Busy roads
1/3 mile on B2146 north of Littlegreen School **6**

Terrain
Several climbs of 100-200ft (30-60m) but this is not as tough a ride as you would expect for one on the South Downs escarpment. One long gentle climb of 255ft (78m) from Littlegreen School up onto the South Downs Way **7** to **8**. One short, steep climb near the end of the ride up to the highpoint in Queen Elizabeth Country Park **11** to **12**

Nearest railway
Petersfield or Rowlands Castle

Refreshments
Café at Queen Elizabeth Country Park Visitor Centre
T: 02392 595040

Chalton
Red Lion PH
T: 02392 592246

Compton (just off route)
Coach & Horses PH
T: 02392 631228

Other rides nearby
There are other waymarked rides from the Queen Elizabeth Country Park Visitor Centre. For other off-road rides in the area see *South East Mountain Biking – North & South Downs* by Nick Cotton

Map pages

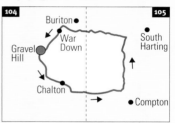

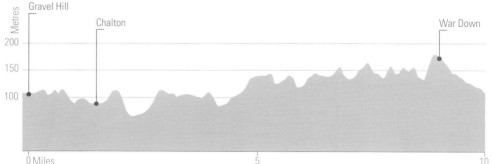

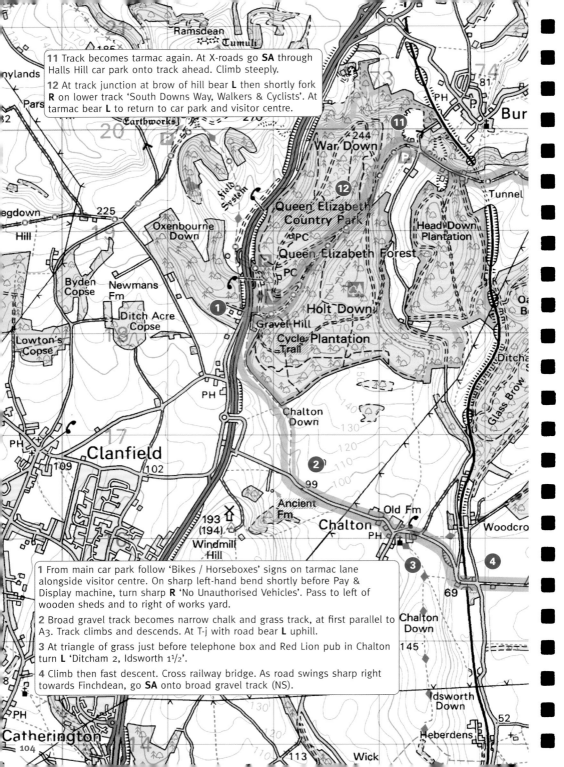

11 Track becomes tarmac again. At X-roads go **SA** through Halls Hill car park onto track ahead. Climb steeply.

12 At track junction at brow of hill bear **L** then shortly fork **R** on lower track 'South Downs Way, Walkers & Cyclists'. At tarmac bear **L** to return to car park and visitor centre.

1 From main car park follow 'Bikes / Horseboxes' signs on tarmac lane alongside visitor centre. On sharp left-hand bend shortly before Pay & Display machine, turn sharp **R** 'No Unauthorised Vehicles'. Pass to left of wooden sheds and to right of works yard.

2 Broad gravel track becomes narrow chalk and grass track, at first parallel to A3. Track climbs and descends. At T-j with road bear **L** uphill.

3 At triangle of grass just before telephone box and Red Lion pub in Chalton turn **L** 'Ditcham 2, Idsworth 1½'.

4 Climb then fast descent. Cross railway bridge. As road swings sharp right towards Finchdean, go **SA** onto broad gravel track (NS).

8 After ¾ mile track turns to tarmac by lovely Foxcombe Farm. After further ¼ mile with red-brick house and barn to right, turn **L** onto broad stone track 'South Downs Way'.

9 At T-j after ¾ mile turn **L** to go past houses 'South Downs Way' then after ½ mile take first lane to **R** by triangle of grass 'South Downs Way' (Ditcham Park School is to left).

10 Follow tarmac as it turns to track and passes beneath power lines. Several ups and downs.

5 Follow this track for almost 2 miles, climbing and descending, ignoring turns to right and left. Go through Cowdown Farm as track turns to concrete then tarmac. At T-j with wider road turn **L** gently downhill.

6 At T-j with B2146 by Littlegreen School turn **L** 'Petersfield, Harting'. Shortly, on right-hand bend, turn **L** 'Bridleway, Hucksholt Farm'. Tarmac soon turns to track.

7 Ignore wide track to left by green gate at end of wood on left. After ½ mile at X-roads with wide stone track go **SA** towards grey metal gate.

Rolling Hampshire downland from New Alresford

This is a real Jekyll and Hyde route. In summer, after a few dry days, it is an easy exploration of the wide tracks that criss-cross this part of Hampshire between hedgerows filled with elderflower, rosehip and willowherb; your worst problem is likely to be the odd nettle or bramble. In winter, or after a few days of heavy rain, it will take you twice as long with big puddles, lots of mud and potentially slippery smooth chalk. The ride leaves the attractive town of New Alresford, soon joining a wide stone-based track that turns to grass, climbing gently through undulating farmland. This is quintessential Hampshire countryside – gently rolling, fine arable country dotted with clumps of broadleaf woodland. A quick look at a map will show you that this is just one of many such rides that radiate out from New Alresford – it really is a case of waiting for the conditions to be right (a long dry spell in summer) then making the most of it. As autumn turns to winter there are ever fewer rideable tracks in this part of England: try staying high on the South Downs ridge, explore local Forestry Commission holdings, be prepared to travel further to the better-draining soils of Exmoor and Dartmoor, to the mountain bike centres in Wales, or why not get a road bike and explore the lanes described in the road rides?

Overview
Off-road ● 12 miles / 19 kilometres ● Easy / Moderate

Start
New Alresford, off the A31 between Winchester and Alton

Parking
Pay & Display car park at New Alresford railway station

Busy roads
The B3046 near New Alresford at the start / finish can get busy

Terrain
Gently undulating. The 295ft (90m) climb in the first half of the ride to Upper Lanham Farm is the only one of note

1 to **5**

Nearest railway
Winchester or Alton

Refreshments
New Alresford
Lots of choice

Other rides nearby
Hampshire County Council produces packs of leaflets with off-road routes – go to www3.hants.gov.uk/cycling and follow links for 'Leaflets and maps'

Map pages

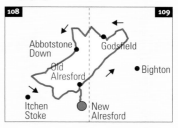

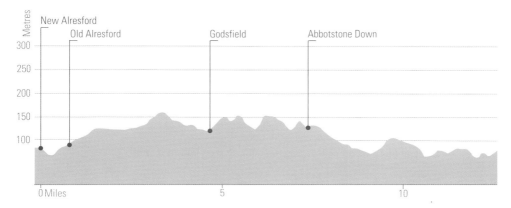

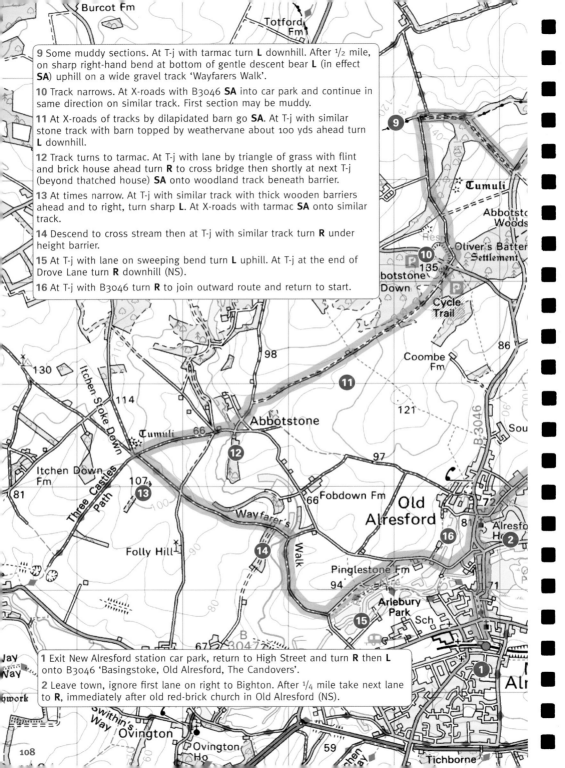

9 Some muddy sections. At T-j with tarmac turn **L** downhill. After ½ mile, on sharp right-hand bend at bottom of gentle descent bear **L** (in effect **SA**) uphill on a wide gravel track 'Wayfarers Walk'.

10 Track narrows. At X-roads with B3046 **SA** into car park and continue in same direction on similar track. First section may be muddy.

11 At X-roads of tracks by dilapidated barn go **SA**. At T-j with similar stone track with barn topped by weathervane about 100 yds ahead turn **L** downhill.

12 Track turns to tarmac. At T-j with lane by triangle of grass with flint and brick house ahead turn **R** to cross bridge then shortly at next T-j (beyond thatched house) **SA** onto woodland track beneath barrier.

13 At times narrow. At T-j with similar track with thick wooden barriers ahead and to right, turn sharp **L**. At X-roads with tarmac **SA** onto similar track.

14 Descend to cross stream then at T-j with similar track turn **R** under height barrier.

15 At T-j with lane on sweeping bend turn **L** uphill. At T-j at the end of Drove Lane turn **R** downhill (NS).

16 At T-j with B3046 turn **R** to join outward route and return to start.

1 Exit New Alresford station car park, return to High Street and turn **R** then **L** onto B3046 'Basingstoke, Old Alresford, The Candovers'.

2 Leave town, ignore first lane on right to Bighton. After ¼ mile take next lane to **R**, immediately after old red-brick church in Old Alresford (NS).

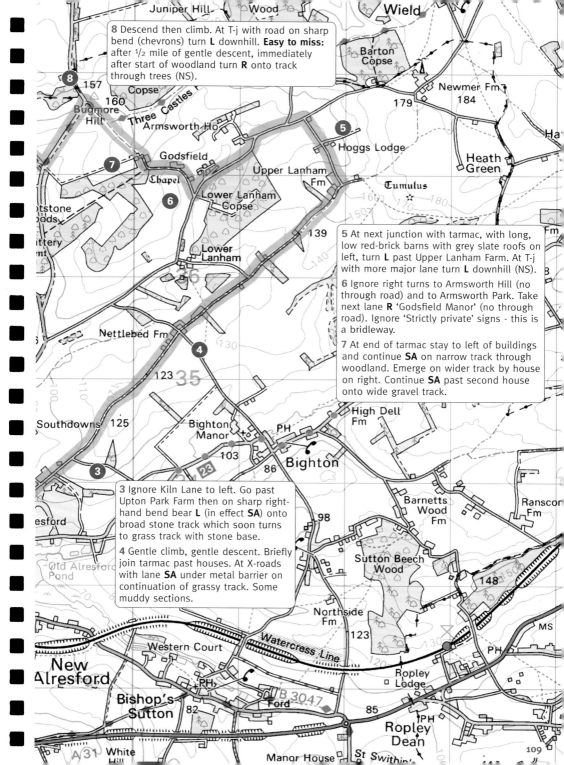

8 Descend then climb. At T-j with road on sharp bend (chevrons) turn **L** downhill. **Easy to miss:** after ½ mile of gentle descent, immediately after start of woodland turn **R** onto track through trees (NS).

5 At next junction with tarmac, with long, low red-brick barns with grey slate roofs on left, turn **L** past Upper Lanham Farm. At T-j with more major lane turn **L** downhill (NS).

6 Ignore right turns to Armsworth Hill (no through road) and to Armsworth Park. Take next lane **R** 'Godsfield Manor' (no through road). Ignore 'Strictly private' signs - this is a bridleway.

7 At end of tarmac stay to left of buildings and continue **SA** on narrow track through woodland. Emerge on wider track by house on right. Continue **SA** past second house onto wide gravel track.

3 Ignore Kiln Lane to left. Go past Upton Park Farm then on sharp right-hand bend bear **L** (in effect **SA**) onto broad stone track which soon turns to grass track with stone base.

4 Gentle climb, gentle descent. Briefly join tarmac past houses. At X-roads with lane **SA** under metal barrier on continuation of grassy track. Some muddy sections.

109

New Forest tracks from Lyndhurst

The New Forest offers some excellent easy off-road cycling but it can also be confusing as so many of the tracks look similar. To solve this problem the Forestry Commission has put in numbered signposts so that in combination with one of their maps (available as a download from www.forestry.gov.uk, search 'New Forest') it is possible to work out any number of routes. Be aware that many of the roads in the New Forest can be quite busy so it is as well to check at each numbered post that you are following a track that will cross a road directly onto another track opposite. This ride moves from the thickly wooded area near Lyndhurst to more open heathland of heather and gorse. On the return half of the ride you may well see many deer in the woods; in addition, of course, to the wild ponies that abound in the area.

Recommended websites for further New Forest rides
www.new-forest-national-park.com
www.forestleisurecycling.co.uk
www.newforestcyclehire.co.uk
www.newforest.gov.uk
www3.hants.gov.uk/cycling/c and click on 'New Forest'
www.forestry.gov.uk/newforest
Search for 'Cycle routes' or 'Cycle maps' to get hold of routes.

Overview

Off-road ● 13 miles / 21 kilometres ● Easy, the easiest off-road ride in the book

Start
Beechen Lane, Lyndhurst. The start is accessed off the A337 Brockenhurst road on the southern edge of Lyndhurst. Beechen Lane is a no through road leading to Hillary Close (opposite the turn to Foxlease)

Parking
Small car park at the end of Beechen Lane

Busy roads
None, unless you choose to divert to visit Brockenhurst

Terrain
Generally flat with only gentle climbs

Nearest railway
Lyndhurst

Refreshments
Lyndhurst
Lots of choice

Brockenhurst, just off the route, follow signs from Forestry Commission Signpost no. 33 / at ❺
Lots of choice

Shortcut
At Instruction 6, instead of going straight ahead, turn left, soon coming to a crossroads by Signpost 39. Turn left here and rejoin at Instructions 14 / 15

Map pages

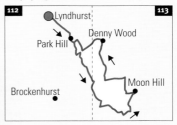

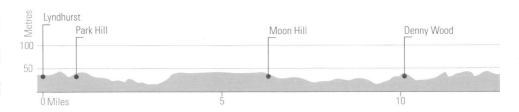

16 At T-j by 'Frohawk' information board turn sharp **R** (3-way signpost). After ½ mile at T-j by 2-way signpost at top of gentle climb turn **L** gently downhill.

17 At next T-j by 3-way sign with Brockenhurst signposted to left, turn **R**. At T-j by Signpost 36 turn **L** 'Lyndhurst' and follow for almost 1 mile, down then up to exit wood back to start.

1 Go **SA** at end of Beechen Lane through gate onto track 'Brockenhurst'.

2 Gentle descent then climb. After 1 mile turn **R** at Signpost 36 'Brockenhurst'.

3 Second gentle descent. At T-j **R** 'Brockenhurst' then after ¼ mile at Signpost No. 35 go **SA** ignoring right turn.

4 Follow main gravel track round sharp left-hand bend. Shortly at Signpost 34 turn **R** 'Brockenhurst 2.5 miles'.

5 Gentle downhill. At Signpost 33 go **SA** onto track with grass growing in middle 'Brockenhurst'. Go through wooden bridlegate next to wooden field gate and follow track round to **R**.

6 At X-roads by Signpost 38 go **SA**. After ¼ mile go through double wooden gates, cross red-brick bridge over railway and go past red-brick houses.

7 At X-roads by 4-way sign go **SA** and after almost ½ mile at X-roads with B3055 go **SA** again 'Forestry Commission Roundhill'.

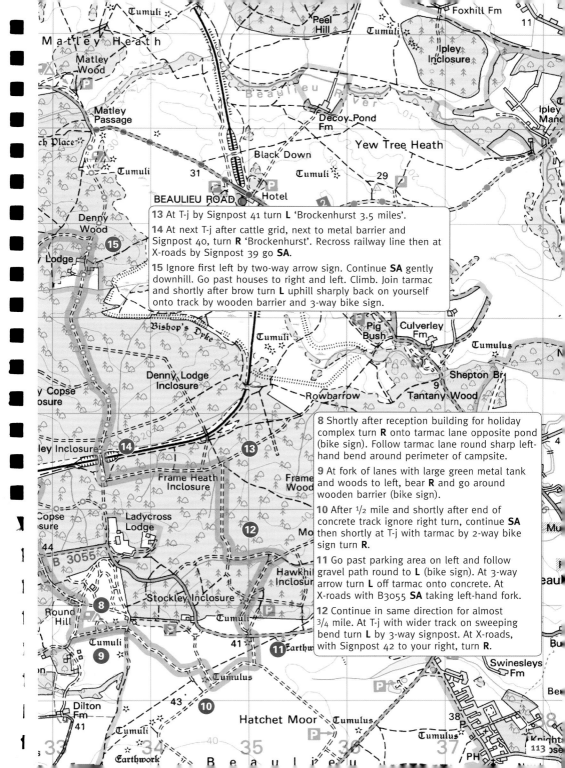

13 At T-j by Signpost 41 turn **L** 'Brockenhurst 3.5 miles'.

14 At next T-j after cattle grid, next to metal barrier and Signpost 40, turn **R** 'Brockenhurst'. Recross railway line then at X-roads by Signpost 39 go **SA**.

15 Ignore first left by two-way arrow sign. Continue **SA** gently downhill. Go past houses to right and left. Climb. Join tarmac and shortly after brow turn **L** uphill sharply back on yourself onto track by wooden barrier and 3-way bike sign.

8 Shortly after reception building for holiday complex turn **R** onto tarmac lane opposite pond (bike sign). Follow tarmac lane round sharp left-hand bend around perimeter of campsite.

9 At fork of lanes with large green metal tank and woods to left, bear **R** and go around wooden barrier (bike sign).

10 After 1/2 mile and shortly after end of concrete track ignore right turn, continue **SA** then shortly at T-j with tarmac by 2-way bike sign turn **R**.

11 Go past parking area on left and follow gravel path round to **L** (bike sign). At 3-way arrow turn **L** off tarmac onto concrete. At X-roads with B3055 **SA** taking left-hand fork.

12 Continue in same direction for almost 3/4 mile. At T-j with wider track on sweeping bend turn **L** by 3-way signpost. At X-roads, with Signpost 42 to your right, turn **R**.

The Tennyson Trail on the Isle of Wight

The wide rollercoaster track known at the Tennyson Trail, which runs along the spine of chalk on the western half of the Isle of Wight, offers some of the finest mountain biking in southern England. The views are stupendous, north across the Solent to the mainland and south across the English Channel. On a fine day there is a tremendous sense of space and if the breeze is up and the sun is out, it is more than likely that the Solent will be filled with brightly coloured yachts. This is the hardest off-road ride in the book with a whole series of climbs, each offering tough challenges on the way up and thrilling descents on the way down. In fact the climbs, descents and views are so good that much of your return route you will retrace your steps back along the Tennyson Trail with spectacular views west towards the Needles. If arriving by ferry in Yarmouth it is easy to pick up a railway path that runs south almost all the way to the start in Freshwater Bay. Another area of the island with a mass of bridleway possibilities lies just inland from the south coast between St Catherine's Hill (near Chale) across to St Martin's Down and Shanklin Down (to the west of Shanklin), taking in the mast on Stenbury Down. Easier off-road trails include the many railway paths that have been converted to recreational use (go to www.cyclewight.org.uk).

Overview
Off-road ● 20 miles / 32 kilometres ● Strenuous

Start
Freshwater Bay, south of Yarmouth at the western end of the Isle of Wight

Parking
Seafront car park in Freshwater Bay

Busy roads
Short climb on A3055 at start

Terrain
Hilly! A series of steep but rideable climbs run along the spine of the island

Nearest ferry
Yarmouth (from Lymington). There is a railway path linking Yarmouth to Freshwater Bay

Refreshments
Freshwater Bay
Lots of choice

Shorwell, just off route at 6
Crown Inn
T: 01983 740293

Shortcut
This is pretty much a linear ride so you can turn around at any point to return to the start

Other rides nearby
The southern half of the island is criss-crossed with well waymarked bridleways so with an Ordnance Survey map it is easy to plan a much longer route, heading southeast towards Ventnor, for example

Map pages

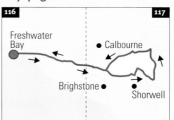

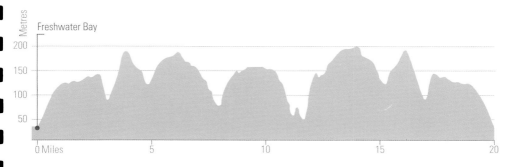

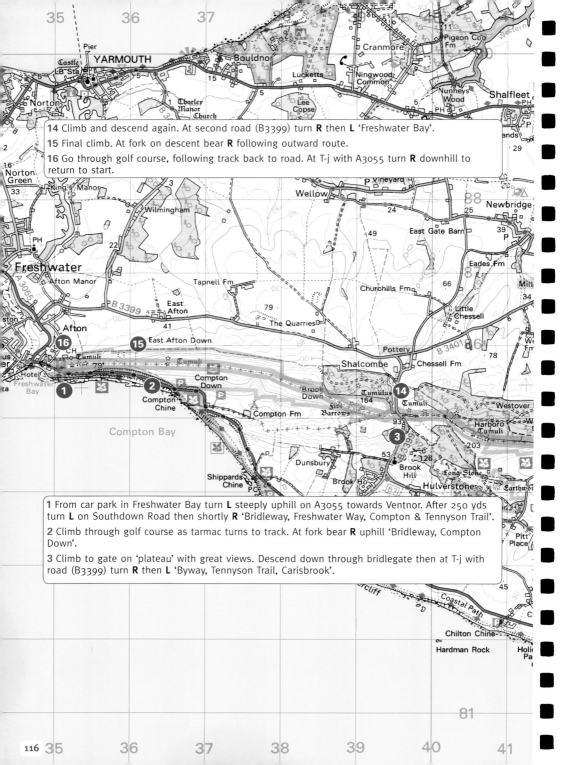

14 Climb and descend again. At second road (B3399) turn **R** then **L** 'Freshwater Bay'.

15 Final climb. At fork on descent bear **R** following outward route.

16 Go through golf course, following track back to road. At T-j with A3055 turn **R** downhill to return to start.

1 From car park in Freshwater Bay turn **L** steeply uphill on A3055 towards Ventnor. After 250 yds turn **L** on Southdown Road then shortly **R** 'Bridleway, Freshwater Way, Compton & Tennyson Trail'.

2 Climb through golf course as tarmac turns to track. At fork bear **R** uphill 'Bridleway, Compton Down'.

3 Climb to gate on 'plateau' with great views. Descend down through bridlegate then at T-j with road (B3399) turn **R** then **L** 'Byway, Tennyson Trail, Carisbrook'.

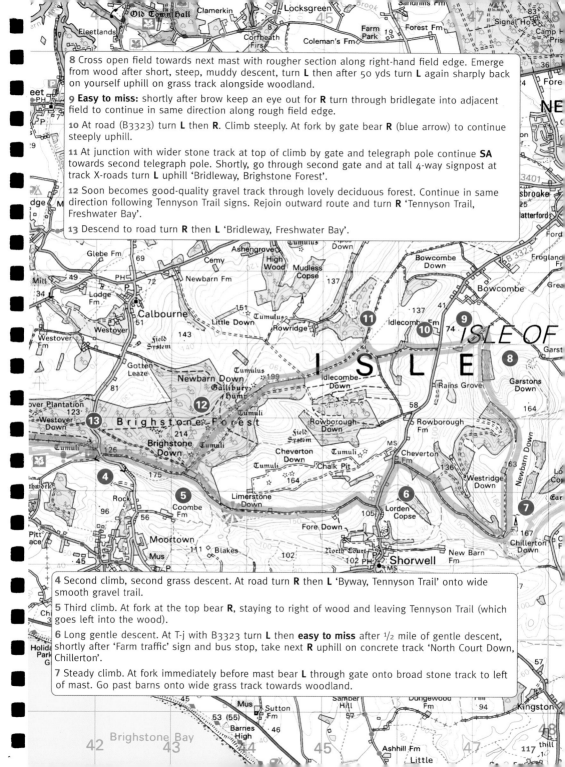

8 Cross open field towards next mast with rougher section along right-hand field edge. Emerge from wood after short, steep, muddy descent, turn **L** then after 50 yds turn **L** again sharply back on yourself uphill on grass track alongside woodland.

9 Easy to miss: shortly after brow keep an eye out for **R** turn through bridlegate into adjacent field to continue in same direction along rough field edge.

10 At road (B3323) turn **L** then **R**. Climb steeply. At fork by gate bear **R** (blue arrow) to continue steeply uphill.

11 At junction with wider stone track at top of climb by gate and telegraph pole continue **SA** towards second telegraph pole. Shortly, go through second gate and at tall 4-way signpost at track X-roads turn **L** uphill 'Bridleway, Brighstone Forest'.

12 Soon becomes good-quality gravel track through lovely deciduous forest. Continue in same direction following Tennyson Trail signs. Rejoin outward route and turn **R** 'Tennyson Trail, Freshwater Bay'.

13 Descend to road turn **R** then **L** 'Bridleway, Freshwater Bay'.

4 Second climb, second grass descent. At road turn **R** then **L** 'Byway, Tennyson Trail' onto wide smooth gravel trail.

5 Third climb. At fork at the top bear **R**, staying to right of wood and leaving Tennyson Trail (which goes left into the wood).

6 Long gentle descent. At T-j with B3323 turn **L** then **easy to miss** after ½ mile of gentle descent, shortly after 'Farm traffic' sign and bus stop, take next **R** uphill on concrete track 'North Court Down, Chillerton'.

7 Steady climb. At fork immediately before mast bear **L** through gate onto broad stone track to left of mast. Go past barns onto wide grass track towards woodland.